When It's Time is a book nobody wants and everyone needs! Finally, there is a resource that has it all. Pastor Rick uses his own life experiences and losses to bring together a collection of the most valuable information that you can ever possess, especially after a significant loss. But the best part is, this book is beyond applicable. When It's Time is practical. My encouragement is to get this book and read it now before you need it.

Dr. Charity M. Byers
CEO and Chief Psychologist
Author of *Unhindered* and *Unhindered Thirty Days*
Blessing Ranch Ministries

Pastor Rick has been my friend and colleague for many years. I know him, respect him, and hold him in the highest regard. He really is one of a kind. His knowledge and expertise on end-of-life issues are beyond comparison. Who knows all this stuff? The answer is, someone who has lived through multiple major losses himself and, in addition, has helped countless others deal with their losses. My encouragement is grab two copies, one for yourself and one for a close friend who needs it NOW.

Dr. John M. Walker
Psychologist and Author

As an Army chaplain for thirty years as well as my time as a VA and hospice chaplain, I have seen the confusion that comes from not knowing what "comes next" after a person dies! Pastor Rick provides a resource that is "over the top" helpful and insightful! When It's Time is an exceptional work that will guide you through the "planning" process at any age, and for survivors after the loss of a loved one. This book is a must read.

Chaplain (COL) Joanne S. Martindale
Army Chaplain, VA Chaplain and Hospice Chaplain

When It's Time is one of the most practical and useful books I wish I had during my public safety career in policing. Over the years I responded to many deaths, both sudden and expected. I watched families struggle with how to manage the difficult details and painful decisions while grieving the loss of their loved one. Thankfully, Pastor Rick Craig has thoughtfully compiled and organized this book as a straightforward guide for anyone to methodically yet compassionately plan or prepare for an end-of-life event. From comprehensive guides to interview questionnaires, and even useful checklist, When It's Time starts the uncomfortable conversation that will guide important and personal decisions whether for you or the ones you love. Most people would prefer to avoid this subject, but everyone needs to read and then use this book.

Chief John Carli, (Ret.)
Vacaville, California Police Department

As a marriage and family therapist, I have access to unlimited resources for my field of practice. When It's Time will be my go-to book for topics concerning planning for end-of-life and survivors navigating through loss of a loved one. Pastor Rick has written a resource that will be a classic in its field. It is a must read!

Tim Frederick, MFT
Napa, California

As a gerontologist, I applaud the concept of end-of-life education that Pastor Rick has defined so well. He teaches us with a servant's heart and applies his personal experience and professional expertise in every chapter for our great benefit. This book is destined to become a beloved, dog-eared textbook by those courageous enough to digest it and put it to work in their own lives. Bravo, Pastor Rick Craig!

Di Patterson, MSG, CPG America's Gerontologist
CEO Success in Aging® Centers, Inc.
dipatterson.com—successinaging.com

WHEN IT'S
TIME™

WHEN IT'S
TIME™

End-of-Life Planning at Any Age:
Make It Part of Your Legacy

Rick Craig

XULON PRESS

Xulon Press
2301 Lucien Way #415
Maitland, FL 32751
407.339.4217
www.xulonpress.com

Cover design: Shawn Montoya and Amanda Wright
Interior design: Michelle Cline

Paperback ISBN-13: 978-1-6628-1557-7
Ebook ISBN-13: 978-1-6628-1558-4

*To the survivors I have worked
with over the years, this book is
dedicated to you. What an
honor it has been to serve you.*

*My prayer for each of you is to find
healing and wholeness again.*

Contents

❧

Foreword . . . .*xi*
Preface . . . . *xiii*
Disclaimer . . . . *xv*
How to Use This Book . . . . *xvii*

Chapter 1   Investigating Life Insurance 1
Chapter 2   Developing Your Estate Plan 17
Chapter 3   Giving the Gift of Organ Donation. 37
Chapter 4   Receiving Hospice Care 55
Chapter 5   Struggling with Sudden Death 69
Chapter 6   Coping with Miscarriage, Stillbirth, and
                     Infant Loss 83
Chapter 7   Clarifying Bereavement Leave 95
Chapter 8   Choosing the Right Funeral Home 109
Chapter 9   Planning a Funeral or Memorial Service 125
Chapter 10   Understanding Your Health Insurance 141
Chapter 11   Applying for Veteran Benefits 151
Chapter 12   Accessing Social Security Benefits 163
Chapter 13   Grieving Your Loss. 175

Afterword—Now It's Time! *191*
Appendix A: Survivor Checklist© *193*
Appendix B: Order of Service Templates *201*
Contributors. *205*
Acknowledgments. *209*
Endnotes. *213*

Foreword

R ick Craig and I have been friends for many years. If there was ever a person who could so beautifully "bind up the brokenhearted . . . comfort all who mourn . . . provide for those who grieve . . . bestow on [the hurting] a crown of beauty" (Isa. 61:1–3 NIV), and help others through despair and devastation, it would be Rick.

Rick has always impressed me by his caring and unconditional love for others, especially when they were suffering a critical event, most often the result of losing their beloved. Rick has spent countless hours on an excellent resource that is sure to provide help to family members, chaplains, clergy, and students, providing the many "next steps" necessary when preparing for and answering end-of-life questions. One of the beauties of this book is that you can begin anywhere to start your plan.

When It's Time is an excellent work that will guide you through a planning process that will be an incredible gift to families and loved ones. As Rick has stated, "Regardless of what it takes to motivate you to get started, take that step today with your family in mind because they will be most grateful!"

—Lee Shaw
Senior Chaplain Napa County Law Enforcement, Fire & EMS Chaplaincy, and United States Secret Service Chaplain

Preface

"What do I do now? We were supposed to be together forever!" The woman I was counseling had just lost her spouse that very morning. As we talked, she revealed not only her pain, distress, and disbelief, but also her grief, compounded by fear—fear stemming from lack of direction. She and her daughter did not know what to do. Could this story also be your story, or that of a relative, friend, or colleague? It doesn't have to end this way, but too often, it does.

End-of-life conversations are not easy for most people. Culturally, the United States has grown less interested in preparing for death. We have no problem planning for life, but death—that's something we'd rather avoid thinking about. As a result, planning for end-of-life often does not receive the same investment as other life priorities, leaving no clear map laid out for navigating the rough terrain ahead. I have learned through both personal and professional experiences that when the person on the opposite side of the table leans toward me and clears his or her throat only to whisper, "What do I do now?" it is a clear indication that little to no time has been spent having those difficult, yet critical, end-of-life conversations. Many do not know how to successfully travel *through* this journey; they simply find themselves traveling *on* the journey, hoping that someone—a confidant, family member, or friend—will walk it with them. But often, that is not enough.

My friend, as you walk this challenging journey, know that I have walked it too. As an ordained Christian pastor trained in this area of ministry, I've officiated more than 150 funerals and memorials and have counseled countless people in pre-need and at-need stages. I've also navigated the loss of several of my own family members. I thank God that I can use my experiences to help others.

The catalyst for this book stems from the loss of my brother and his disappointing funeral service as the result of poor planning. In contrast, my wife's memorial service was attended by more than 200 people from around the globe. My mom passed away six months later followed with a simple, yet honoring memorial service. Ten years after my mom's death, my dad passed, and the way we honored him and memorialized his legacy will live on in our hearts.

To present the best guidance possible, I have called upon professionals in various fields to co-author this book with me. I will introduce their contributions in each chapter. For more information about these contributing authors, see the Contributor section at the end of this book. Please allow us the privilege of guiding you through this process with the hope of easing some of the more practical burdens so you can truly honor and memorialize your loved one. View this book as a map, with the starting point being wherever you are today in this journey, pointing you down a path that is well-worn, yet seldom revealed.

Disclaimer

A s you read this book, at no time should you take my suggestions, or those of the contributing authors, as absolute
directives and act upon them as such. While each chapter is filled
with valuable information that you can apply to many situations,
it is offered only as helpful suggestions. I encourage you to seek
the advice of professionals in each field, since your situation may
differ from mine and others I have worked with. Your state laws
may be different than mine in California, and your circumstances
will certainly not mirror mine nor those I have worked with in
every scenario. Please take this information, my story, and the
stories of others as examples only, not legal advice to help you
address your specific needs.

I have no legal, financial, or marketing relationship with any of
the resources listed in this book. These resources are listed solely
for your reference and education. Many websites are available to
the reader, and I encourage you to do your own research.

How to Use This Book

*W*hen *It's Time* will introduce and highlight thirteen topics to consider for end-of-life arrangements. Whether life insurance, trusts and wills, organ donation, funeral/memorial services, veteran's benefits, or employee bereavement leave, this is your guidebook. I have authored this book with two readers in mind: those who are **"pre-need"** *planners making plans in advance for their own end-of-life*, and those who are **"at-need"** *survivors dealing with the death of a loved one*.

If end-of-life is not imminent and you are planning pre-need, I encourage you to read this book in chronological order. By doing so, you will find a systematic approach on how to prepare for your or a loved one's end-of-life. You will soon learn that the process involves more than just planning a funeral or memorial service. You will begin to develop a team of family members, friends, business partners, and professionals, such as funeral directors, financial planners, attorneys, insurance agents, medical professionals, tax preparers, and work colleagues, who will each have a role in your end-of-life plan. I have learned that planning early in life—especially if you have a young family, a family with one income earner, or are a single person of age—is a tremendous gift that you leave for your surviving family. It is never too late to offer this expression of love to your survivors.

On the other hand, if you are a reader who is at-need due to the recent death of a loved one, then jump to the chapters that address your current place in the process. In these cases, you may only have hours or days to become equipped. The content is meant to assist you at your very moment of need. You will still have to build a team of people to assist you, so reading the applicable chapters associated with your journey will be your best plan of action. Also, make sure to check out the "Survivor's Checklist©" in the appendix. This invaluable resource will guide you through the days following the loss of a loved one.

As a pastor, I see the value of planning for the inevitability of death each time I sit with survivors after the loss of a loved one. Those who pre-plan for end-of-life give their survivors an incredible gift. The time they invested in planning allows survivors to grieve without the anxiety-producing guesswork. When I meet with survivors of someone who pre-planned, we talk about their loved one's legacy and the impact it has made. As they share stories about their loved one (frequently causing a good belly laugh), the conversation turns to the deceased's character traits, personal values, convictions, and contributions to society. After a while, our discourse becomes more focused on the details of the service, my role as the officiant, and the focus of the message.

Conversely, when I sit with the family of someone who has not planned for end-of-life, or if the death has occurred suddenly and without the option of pre-planning, the questions are noticeably different. Initially, the questions by the at-need survivors involve the financial aspect of a funeral or memorial. Then the deliberation begins: cremation versus casket, location of burial, venue for the service, speakers, music, food, and more. The list of questions consumes our time together and continues over the phone for a couple of days. Without pre-planning, the at-need survivors are not only grieving their loss, but they are also thrust into decision-making that is exhausting, and quite often, it entails *guessing* what the deceased would have wanted versus *knowing* what to do.

When It's Time is your comprehensive guide for this inevitable journey. Some chapters will address pre-need topics, some will address at-need topics, and some will address both. Chapters addressing both will be divided by pre-need and at-need headings for easy reference. At the end of each chapter is a section titled "Action Steps." These action steps capture key points in each chapter, offering you a beginning point. These action steps can also equip you to have conversations with family members and professionals as part of planning. Since end-of-life conversations tend to be difficult, having common talking points to discuss can help start the process. Lastly, some action steps will encourage a time of reflection as you determine your own last wishes.

Whether you are reading this book pre-need or at-need, you have made a conscious choice that will place you well ahead of others when making end-of-life decisions. I encourage you to share your progress with your family or those closest to you who will be part of your team. End-of-life conversations can be challenging, but also rewarding. My most heartfelt professional encouragement for you is this: Start the journey now, and let it be part of your legacy!

WHEN IT'S TIME™

CHAPTER 1

Investigating Life Insurance

I n early 1992, Susie, my wife-to-be, and I were playing our weekly game of tennis. She was in great physical condition and played tennis two or three times a week, in addition to daily walks. However, her energy level had changed drastically over the last few weeks, and before we had even finished the first set, she was exhausted and had to sit down and rest. After a few minutes of rest, she said, "I'm done." My immediate response was, "You need to make a doctor's appointment to find out what's going on!" I don't recall the number of days before she was seen by her doctor for a check-up, but it happened quickly. After her second doctor's appointment, which happened in rapid succession, she called me, panicked. "I have breast cancer," she said. She was in shock, and so was I.

We married in November 1993 after a long treatment period using the latest and best medical protocols for first-time breast cancer patients. It appeared to be working until the five-year mark. On that five-year anniversary day—the day I was throwing a party to celebrate her good health—she got a phone call from her oncologist, saying, "Your cancer has returned, and it has metastasized into your bone." This startling diagnosis began a ten-year battle for her life, a battle that tested us in many ways, and a battle that enabled me to help others along the way—even today.

Approximately one week before her five-year "remission celebration," Susie had obtained life insurance. She wanted both of her sisters—her older sister had health issues, and her younger sister has suffered from polio and post-polio since she was six weeks old—to be financially sound upon reaching end-of-life. We had been covering all costs associated with her sister's post-polio condition and everyday living expenses. So, in this small window of opportunity, Susie took out a life insurance policy, naming her sisters as beneficiaries. It wasn't until later that we learned just how much a gift this was. Ten years after the cancer recurred, Susie died. But because of her prudence and persistence in obtaining life insurance, her sisters were left financially secure.

How does this story pertain to you? The answer is simple. You never know if you will qualify for life insurance tomorrow. Procrastination could leave you uninsurable. I share my story not to frighten you, but to encourage you. Investigating your insurance coverage needs sooner rather than later is prudent. To best answer questions on the need for life insurance and how much is enough, I turn to my good friend Barrie Sandy, an insurance agent who sells home, auto, life and business insurance in Vallejo, California. Here is Barrie's guidance on life insurance.

Pre-Need

Why Do I Need Life Insurance?

Everyone has different needs when it comes to life insurance. Unless you have already won the financial game and your assets or estate can provide for your heirs long after you reach end-of-life, buying life insurance is always a good idea.

Most people seek out life insurance stemming from a notable life event, such as marriage or divorce, the birth of children, purchasing a home, starting a new job, or building a new business. When purchasing a life insurance policy, you will assess your needs, determine a benefit amount, and review coverage periodically to ensure the policy amount continues to meet your needs. It is generally very affordable unless you have a serious pre-existing medical condition or have been previously found ineligible for a life insurance policy. Even then, there may still be ways you can get some life insurance coverage through a no-exam policy, a mortgage life insurance policy, or some other types of policies. Here are the most common reasons to buy life insurance:

To Provide for Survivors

If you're on the fence about buying life insurance, think about what it would mean to your survivors if you were to die without a life insurance policy in place.

- Would they be in a good place from a financial standpoint?
- Could they continue living their lives with the same standard of living?
- Would they have to downsize their home, sell their possessions, skip out on college, or be burdened with substantial student loan debt?
- Would they be saddled with final expenses, such as medical bills or funeral expenses?
- Would they have to change their life plans—go back to work, take a second job, or work longer before retiring?

Most people who ask themselves these questions generally find they absolutely need a life insurance policy. Having a policy provides peace of mind, knowing that your family will be covered should you die.

To Cover Final Expenses

Even when no one is relying upon your income for support, *someone* will be paying for your final expenses. Medical bills and funeral expenses can easily cost thousands of dollars, and while medical insurance helps, it may not cover everything. If you type "burial cost" or related terms into your computer's search engine, you will find a plethora of information on the average cost for funerals and cremation. Funeral costs could range starting from $10,000 or more, based on where you live and the services/components you choose. The average cost of a funeral with cremation is less, although still expensive. And these costs do not include a cemetery, monument/marker, flowers, officiant, reception, and so on. Beyond the cost for the funeral and burial, there may also be additional expenses, such as providing meals for family and other attendees.

Some people choose to buy a burial insurance policy or "final expense" insurance. These are whole life insurance policies that are typically $25,000 or less in the policy's face amount of coverage. While a final expense policy may be helpful, it may not be adequate for the family's other financial needs.

I remember a recent conversation with a customer who requested enough life insurance to cover a $30,000 funeral she was anticipating for herself because that was the approximate cost for her mother's recent funeral, burial, and food expenses for their large, extended family who traveled from out of town. While there was a final expense policy in place for her mother, it was not nearly enough to cover the entire expense, so close family members were expected to come up with the balance. Those conversations are not easy to have, and they can create a financial burden while adding stress to family relationships.

> *Rick's Story*
> *As a pastor officiating services in the Bay Area of Northern California, my experience has been that the average cost of a funeral/memorial is considerably higher than the median cost for the country as a whole. Evaluating the anticipated cost for your location is paramount in determining how much burial insurance you need. In addition, if the deceased is being transported outside of your geographical area for burial, the costs rise dramatically; therefore, it is wise to factor in potential additional costs when planning.*
>
> *When Susie died, her wish was to be cremated, as stipulated in our trust, and this was faithfully fulfilled. We hired a licensed boat out of Bodega Bay to spread her ashes at sea. There were just six of us*

on the boat allowing us to have a small, intimate ceremony. A few weeks later we held a service at our church with over 200 people in attendance. At that time in 2007, the total cost for both cremation and burial at sea was around $1,600. When compared to having a funeral with a casket, plot, service, and other related expenses, cremation was a fraction of the price of burial. Although Susie's choice for cremation was not based on cost, this example shows that honorable memorials and burials do not always have to be expensive. There is a choice.

It is important to understand that the size of the policy affects how long it takes to receive the payout. Larger policies can take longer to pay out. Following the underwriting process, there is a two-year contestable period entitling the insurance company to review and confirm your original application. This could delay your payment for up to sixty days. Because of this, having a smaller final expense policy in place helps beneficiaries receive immediate cash once a certified death certificate is available.

During the first two years of many final expense policies, the death benefit paid to the beneficiary is limited to 110 percent of the premiums due and paid, unless the insured's death is due to accidental bodily injury, as defined in the contract. This depends on the health of the insured at the time the policy is enforced. If the insured is in good health, some carriers offer policies with smaller payout amounts (with smaller premiums that can fit tighter budgets) that give them immediate coverage without a two-year wait period for the beneficiary to receive full face value upon the decedent's death.

To Replace a Primary Income

Obtaining a policy for the primary income earner in a family should be given serious consideration. Most families would not be able to pay their regular bills without the monthly income of the primary earner. A well-planned life insurance policy would cover the outstanding balance on a mortgage and leave enough to help pay for living expenses for the next twenty years, or until the spouse would be able to start making penalty-free withdrawals from retirement accounts.

To Cover the Cost of a Spouse's Contributions

It is a good idea to have life insurance coverage on a stay-at-home spouse, even if his or her income is low or non-existent. Stay-at-home spouses often contribute in a wide variety of ways, including childcare, running the household, cooking, cleaning, and many other necessary duties. You might be able to provide for your own home responsibilities, but having the financial means to hire help when needed can make a huge difference. This is especially important if you have children who are too young to attend school.

To Pay for Children's Expenses

This includes childcare and other school-age needs, such as activities, sports, music, tutoring, and anticipated college or trade school expenses. College or trade school may be years in the future, or it might be right around the corner. Either way, it can be extremely expensive. Having a life insurance policy may mean the difference between your child attending college or trade school without worrying about the cost versus skipping college or taking out large student loans.

To Pay Off Any Outstanding Debts

Debt can look different for everyone, especially if there is consumer debt. When there is a mortgage, the question I like to ask is, "Do you want to leave your surviving spouse with the *debt* or the *deed*?" As I mentioned above, an adequate policy will be enough to pay off the loan balance and still have enough left over for bridging the gap between now and retirement. But each situation is different, so it is important to look at any outstanding debts and consider that amount when determining how much life insurance is needed. Being able to pay off all debts would give your family a fresh start when end-of-life occurs.

To Pay for Long-Term Care for Children with Special Needs

If your income is needed to support dependents long after you retire, you should consider a large life insurance policy. This could include a child or someone else with special needs who will not be able to support him or herself. In this case, you'll want to look at a "whole" life insurance policy over a "term" life insurance policy (more on that below). In addition to life insurance, you should research a special needs trust through an attorney specializing in this area. State and federal benefits for children with special needs can be put at risk upon the inheritance of assets that supersede the agency's allowed levels, disqualifying them from critically needed services. Planning a special needs trust in tandem with life insurance will ensure your child's continued financial stability and keep his or her services and benefits intact.

To Buy Out a Business Partner's Interest

Many business partners take out a life insurance policy on their partners to ensure a more stable transition in the event that one of the partners passes away while the business is still operating. This is often coupled with a buy-sell agreement that is triggered in the event of one partner's death. Strategically, it can help the business continue without trying to find a buyer for either the entire business or the deceased partner's shares. It also prevents the heirs from dealing with a business when there is little interest or adequate knowledge. This can be a complicated topic and is worth exploring with the assistance of a legal consultant who specializes in small or large businesses.

To Cover Estate Taxes

Estate taxes are expensive and can eat away a large percentage of an heir's inheritance. Many high net-worth individuals use life insurance as an estate planning tool and a way to mitigate the cost of their estate taxes. Again, this is a more advanced topic and one that is worth consulting with an estate lawyer. This is also one of the few times that whole life insurance is recommended over a term life insurance policy.

What Type of Life Insurance Should I Purchase?

There are two main types of life insurance policies: whole and term.

Whole life insurance lasts for your entire life, provided you "keep the policy in force" (stay current with the premiums). Whole life insurance premiums are significantly more expensive than term life insurance premiums for the same amount of coverage. Many life insurance agents peddle whole life insurance as an investment. It is not a good investment. Life insurance and investing should never be mixed. Life insurance should only be used as life insurance. However, there are times when whole life insurance is the best form of life insurance for a specific person or situation, such as when you will need the life insurance proceeds for your heirs, regardless of your age when you reach end-of-life. Two common examples were previously mentioned: caring for a dependent with special needs and estate planning. These are situations when the higher life insurance premiums are worth paying for to have a permanent policy that never expires.

Term life insurance only lasts for the term of the policy (often issued in ten, twenty, or thirty-year periods) and is recommended for most common life insurance needs. Premiums are less expensive for the same policy value as whole life insurance, and most people do not need a life insurance policy for their entire lives. If you have planned well throughout your life, your need for insurance will decrease as you age since fewer people are relying upon your income to support them. Many people find they can go without life insurance after they reach a certain stage in life, often at or near retirement. Prior to that, their financial needs are often greater—paying a mortgage, supporting a family, sending kids to college, saving for retirement, and so on. But financial needs are reduced once children have left the home, the mortgage is paid off, and you are no longer saving for retirement. A term life policy is a good solution for life insurance needs that follow this path.

Most major life insurance companies offer their term life insurance products at a minimum coverage amount of $100,000. A few will go as low as $25,000–$50,000. Premium rates for these smaller covered amounts tend to be higher per unit than those for larger coverage amounts (a unit equals $1,000 of coverage). Therefore, consumers interested in smaller policies should also review quotes for policies at the $100,000 coverage amount since the premium rates may actually be similar. These small policies are attractive because you can apply online or by phone without having to take a paramedical exam. Coverage is usually approved or declined on the spot, and the policy can be paid for and put in force within minutes. This type of term life insurance is commonly referred to as instant issue term or simplified issue term.

> *Rick's Story*
> *When we bought the policy on Susie during that brief opportunity before her second cancer diagnosis, we purchased term life insurance. We chose a term life policy because it cost much less than a whole life policy, and we knew her diagnosis meant life expectancy beyond thirty years was unlikely. This was a hard process mentally and emotionally for us, but we forced ourselves to be pragmatic about our decisions.*

There are other types of life insurance, but many of them are overly complicated. More complication means added expense, regardless of whether it provides added value. Unfortunately, added expense also equals increased commissions, so some life insurance sales agents try to push these complicated insurance policies because the commission is higher. Find your needs and then work from there. Do not let a sales agent talk you into buying something you do not need.

How Much Life Insurance Should You Buy?

This is a big topic and one that does not have a one-size-fits-all answer. There are several rules of thumb, such as ten times annual income. But those rules of thumb can be overkill or woefully inadequate, depending on your situation. A better way to approach this is to consider what your survivors' expenses will be after you reach end-of-life. If your goal is to help your survivors maintain their current quality of life, consider factors such as your current debt (mortgage, cars, student loans, and other loans) and expected costs for dependents (daycare age through high school, extracurricular activities, college tuition, and living expenses). Now consider how much of your income would have been used to support the family and additional expenses. This should be enough to get you started with the brainstorming process while you consider which "riders" (optimal coverages for a nominal cost) you might want to add to your policy.

Any life insurance is helpful, but it would be better to have adequate rather than inadequate life insurance. "Stacking" life insurance policies is becoming a common practice. For example, you can start with a thirty-year term life insurance policy. As your needs grow, you can add another twenty-year policy, then a ten-year policy, or any combination to extend coverage. Review your needs to determine if this is a good option for you, and get quotes from at least two or three life insurance providers to find the best policy.

> *Rick's Story*
> *After Susie and I were married, we purchased a home, but within a few months, I lost my job when the company sold. Susie's income provided for our basic living expenses and financial help for her sisters. After a short period of unemployment, I started my own company. It took nearly a*

year to become profitable, but it was not profitable enough to purchase additional life insurance. Due to Susie's re-diagnosis, the window to increase her coverage had closed because she was now uninsurable. In hindsight, we should have made additional cutbacks on our spending and purchased additional life insurance. Fortunately, we were diligent in buying life insurance; unfortunately, we did not buy enough.

Should You Take Out Life Insurance on Your Children?

The question of whether to buy life insurance for children sparks strong debate about the value of such policies. Life insurance for children is often marketed to parents or grandparents to save money for kids and to "protect their insurability," meaning their chance to buy more life insurance later, no matter their health. For these reasons, some life insurance agents say purchasing life insurance on a child can be a smart financial move, but many financial advisors caution against it because they struggle to see how it makes sense.

Most insurance agents and financial advisors can agree on one point: essential financial foundations should come first before you even think about buying a life insurance policy on a child. Those include building an adequate emergency savings fund, making sure parents have enough life and disability insurance, building savings for the child's college tuition (life insurance can be a good vehicle for college savings), and getting your own retirement savings on track.

There are a couple of ways to buy life insurance on a child who is a minor. You can buy coverage on your child's life via a term life insurance policy covering yourself or your spouse. You do this by buying a rider (an extra policy feature at added cost) that extends a small amount, such as $20,000, in life insurance to other family members, including children. Term life insurance pays a death benefit to the beneficiary if the insured person dies during the term. This is the only way to buy term life insurance on a child; there are no standalone term life insurance policies for minors. Most lenders require that the child's life insurance amount be 50 percent or less of the parent's policy.

Alternatively, you can buy a whole life insurance policy covering your child. These are generally for small face amounts, such as $50,000 or less. Permanent life insurance includes a savings account that gradually builds value over time. A parent or grandparent can make a child the policy owner once the child reaches adulthood. Getting a whole life insurance policy for your child now is a good idea for the following reasons:

Affordable Premiums

Kids are generally young and healthy, which means they will get lower life insurance rates. If a child develops a medical problem early in life, he or she might have trouble qualifying for coverage later. By purchasing coverage now, you guarantee the child has some coverage and may even be able to buy more as an adult, regardless of health.

Cash Value

The savings component of a permanent life insurance policy, called cash value, grows tax-deferred. The policy owner can borrow against the cash value (loan interest is added to loan balance) or surrender the policy for the money (minus a possible surrender fee), and if you only make a partial withdrawal, it will diminish the face value of the policy. The cash could be used for anything, including college expenses or the down payment on a home. A whole life insurance policy guarantees a certain percentage return on the cash value and compares well with other conservative savings vehicles like CDs. It is not designed to be a primary savings and investment tool, but it is something for parents and grandparents to consider.

Final Expenses

In the tragic event of a child's death, a life insurance payout could pay for funeral expenses, family counseling, medical bills, and provide money for the family to get by if the parents need to take leave from work. Because they are smaller policies, they generally pay out sooner (with a valid death certificate), so they can be available for the purpose intended—burial costs.

At-Need

Handling a Life Insurance Claim after Death

Locating and handling life insurance claims are not typically a required part of settling an estate as an executor. Why? Because in most cases, life insurance is a non-probate asset. This means the insurance payment will not be made to the deceased's estate but rather directly to the beneficiary or beneficiaries listed on the life insurance policy. However, since the executor is going through paperwork and organizing documents, it is often practical to include handling the life insurance claim as part of your executor's duties. So, what does the executor need to know? Here are answers to four common questions about handling life insurance as an estate executor.

How Do I Know If the Deceased Had a Life Insurance Policy?

This can be the hardest part of the job. Often, people buy life insurance policies and forget about them, sticking the paperwork in a long-forgotten file folder or safety deposit box. As a result, you will want to get into detective mode and look everywhere you can think of. Go through paperwork carefully and review checking and savings accounts for transactions with an insurance company. Did the deceased have other insurance coverage, for example, car or home insurance? If so, they might have also purchased life insurance from the same insurance agent, so reaching out to the agent is a worthwhile step. You also may want to check with the deceased's employer(s) to see if any life insurance benefits are available. Also, many banks and credit unions carry small policies for their members, so check with the banking institution they are affiliated with to see if the decedent had one in force.

> *Rick's Story*
> *Since I was the executor of Susie's estate, I knew I had to set up a filing system while she was going through her medical treatments and acquiring life insurance. Organization was a necessity due to the number of medical bills and amount of paperwork involved. I had anticipated that one day I would be forced to handle these affairs upon her death, operating in a state of shock with my mental capacity greatly diminished as I grieved. I did not realize how prophetic this thought was at the time. I came to realize how important it was to maintain accurate and accessible records—both for me and other family members who would be helping me.*

How Do I Know If the Life Insurance Policy Is Part of the Estate or Not?

In general, if the life insurance policy lists a beneficiary who is living, the policy is entirely separate from the estate. The beneficiary will be paid by the insurance company and can do whatever he or she wishes with the money. However, if the deceased left the proceeds from the life insurance policy to his or her own estate, then the money will be considered estate assets and part of the probate process. What does this mean? It means that if the deceased has outstanding bills and debts at the time he or she dies, then as executor, you might be forced to use some of the insurance proceeds to cover those debts. After any debts are settled, the remaining life insurance monies will go to the beneficiaries listed in the trust or will, along with any other assets.

If no one is listed as the policy's beneficiary, or the person listed is already deceased, one of two scenarios typically happens:

The life insurance proceeds become part of the deceased's estate, or the insurance proceeds bypass the estate and go directly to the deceased's "heirs-at-law." Heirs-at-law are people closely related, and in most cases, would be considered legal heirs even if someone left no will at all. Keep in mind that state laws and insurance company policies can vary here, so the processes can vary also.

> *A Note from Rick*
> *If a diagnosis is made of potential or imminent death, the employee or family member should contact his or her human resources department and obtain information on a life insurance policy, if available. Remember, if the policy is old and beneficiaries have changed, but the policy does not reflect these changes, it is too late after death to change the policy. In addition, having knowledge of the policy's dollar value will assist the survivors in funeral/memorial preparation.*

What If the Insurance Company that Holds the Policy Is No Longer in Business?

Many of the older and smaller insurance companies have been bought or merged with larger companies over the years. As a result, it can be tough to figure out which company currently holds a policy. If you are not certain, contact the appropriate state department of insurance, and in most cases, they can help you.

How Long Does It Take for a Life Insurance Claim to Be Paid?

You will need a death certificate to file a claim and obtaining those can take a couple of weeks or longer after someone dies. Once you have the death certificate and file the claim, the money is typically paid within two to four weeks. While this chapter covers the most common life insurance questions, you may have others if you are an executor. In that case, it would be advisable to reach out to an estate attorney or trusted adviser if the executor is unsure how to handle any of his or her executor duties. Equipped with the proper information, you can be confident that you are doing the job correctly and following all legal requirements.

Action Steps

- If you are considering buying life insurance, schedule a meeting with two or three agents to assess your needs and budget.
- If you already have life insurance, make an appointment with your agent to review your coverage and make any necessary changes.
- Review your current designated beneficiaries and make changes if needed.
- If you are making an insurance claim after someone has died, contact your insurance agent for assistance.

CHAPTER 2

Developing Your Estate Plan

"**P**lan your dive and dive your plan!"
In the mid-1970s, I became a certified scuba diver. My instructor repeated that same phrase every time we met. He drilled into our minds the critical importance of planning the details of our dive (location, depth, and duration) and sharing it with another person who would stay behind. Why? Because if we didn't return at the anticipated time, the designated person would alert the authorities that something was wrong. Based on our dive plan, the rescue team would know exactly where to begin their search. If a diver deviated from the plan without alerting the support person, then the search party would likely start searching in the wrong area, wasting valuable lifesaving time. That phrase, "Plan your dive and dive your plan," has stuck with me ever since, and I have applied it to many of life's scenarios with success. The same fundamentals of the dive plan apply to end-of-life planning: develop a plan, inform a trusted person about it, and live it out!

When Susie and I were newlyweds in 1993, the two of us met with a financial advisor to discuss our portfolio. The company I worked for at the time offered a generous 401k program, and the CFO was excellent at offering financial advice to employee participants. Since I was in senior management, I was fortunate to have extra time with our CFO, gleaning more knowledge about investing. Based on my resolve in saving, coupled with the fact that the stock market was doing well, I felt rather good about my financial investments thus far. So, when Susie and I met with this new financial advisor, it was my first experience with financial planning outside of my company plan.

Our new financial advisor, who worked for one of the big investment firms, gave us the clear impression that our financial future looked bright: "Just keep doing what you are doing, and you will retire early and enjoy life!" he said. But you know what they say about things sounding too good to be true . . .

Over the course of the next fifteen years, not only did our family dynamics change, but so did the financial market. The financial crisis of 2008 delivered a significant blow to my retirement savings and property value. Many of you may still be feeling the sting of this financial crash as well. Following the financial crisis, I diversified my remaining assets and worked diligently to become debt-free. I cannot say it was easy. I made major lifestyle adjustments, managed to cut back on expenses, and ultimately became free of debt. The liberation of carrying no debt is something I strive to maintain. That is not to say I will never have a modest car payment in the future, but if/when that time comes, I will make extra payments to shorten the life of the loan and return to being debt-free.

I am a firm believer in developing teams when the topic in question is not your area of expertise. Is this humility or logic speaking? Hopefully, both! In my financial recovery and planning, I called on a few individuals to help me. One of them was my longtime friend and financial advisor/investor Kent Kuhlmann of Napa, California. Here is Kent's guidance on the importance of financial planning, wills, and trusts.

Pre-Need

Developing Financial and Legal Plans for End-of-Life

As a financial professional and wealth advisor for nearly thirty years, I have walked many people through the various financial challenges and transitions that we all face during our lifetime. Most of these are not necessarily planned for, and as such, we are thrown into situations that are both urgent and complex when we may not be in a good mental, emotional, or physical state to engage properly. There are few things in life that have a more significant financial impact on us than the loss of a loved one.

I learned a valuable lesson about the importance of planning when my (Kent's) mother died years ago. My father was incapable of dealing with virtually anything, so it became my job to step in as trustee and manage his financial affairs after her death. Since I had accompanied my parents to the meeting with their attorney when their trust was developed, I was familiar with their estate plan. Still, even knowing this and understanding how the system works, I was astonished at how much work it was—even for someone who had been down that road so many times with clients. Therefore, with confidence and experience, I can say it is critical to have trusted help in this situation, and hopefully, this chapter will serve as a guide, assisting you through this process. Although we never want to think about these things happening, it is critical to do some type of planning because it is not "if" we are going to leave this life, but "when."

> One of the greatest gifts you can give your children and heirs is a well-planned estate.

History is littered with the chaos that ensues following an end-of-life that has not been carefully planned. Every day, we see headlines of famous people who die without a proper plan in place. After the fights in court and paying the attorneys, there is little money left. Even for those who do plan, unless it is done well, it can be all for naught, as an ambiguous plan can result in the same chaotic outcome as described above. Over the years, I have counseled people who would tell me, "Oh, our kids all love each other and get along." While this may be the case while you are alive, I can testify that about 95 percent of the time, there are issues when mom and dad pass. If there is any part of your plan left "for the kids to figure out," I would urge you to nail it down now.

Rick's Story
*After Susie and I developed our trust, my dad
and mom followed suit. The idea was that with a
trust in place, upon their deaths, my brother and I
would be spared from potential family disputes and
allowed to simply grieve. Even though my family
got along, we all know issues can arise unexpectedly when dealing with estate distributions. I can
attest to the benefits of financial planning, which
include developing a will and trust.*

Wills and Trusts

Creating a will or trust is never a favorite task to think about
or implement. It involves some critical thinking and perhaps challenging decision-making, not to mention the financial expense of
having a will and trust drafted. However, as soon as you begin
accumulating assets, get married, and especially if you have children, you should have a plan in place. We all like to think we
will be around and healthy forever, but the only constant in life is
change. And as we all know . . . stuff happens. If you find yourself needing guidance in this area, below are some planning tools
to help you get started.

The Benefits of Wills and Trusts

I am not an attorney, but due to the nature of my business, I
have dealt with clients' wills and trusts countless times over the
years. While I will not get into the specifics of how these documents are written or what they do, I can share some helpful
insights. I am often asked, "Do I need a trust?" My answer is generally yes. However, this is predicated on your financial status, the
complexity of your family and financial life, and where you live.
If you have minor children, you at least need a will, and generally,
if you own a home or other substantial assets, you need a trust.

A trust is a legal vehicle that holds your assets "in trust." Having your assets held in a trust does not change much while you are alive since you are the trustee and still have control over everything. But having a trust does provide certain tax advantages and establishes the framework of governing the disposition of your assets after your death. This becomes critical in today's world of multiple marriages and blended families. Another benefit of having a trust is to keep your estate transition private as opposed to only having a will and going through the lengthy, public, and expensive process of probate.

Taking the necessary steps to avoid probate is strongly encouraged. Why? First, it is a public proceeding. Anyone can easily find out the details of your estate and proceedings online, which contains personal details of assets, family members, and more. Second, one of the primary purposes of probate is to give creditors the opportunity to have their debts settled with the decedent. Once creditors are notified of a death, they simply file a claim, creating hassles and delays in settling the estate. Third, if you have children under the age of eighteen but no will or trust, the probate court will decide who will take care of your children, and it is not always the most logical or ideal solution. The process is fraught with rules and procedures that must be followed, and court approvals must be obtained for each step. It is not unusual for this process to carry on for years in some cases. Finally, probate usually involves significant attorney's fees, which are charged as a percentage of the value of the estate. In California, for example, the fees to administer a simple estate with a single property valued at $700,000 would start at $21,000. Of course, any complications that arose could cause it to climb well beyond that.

Benefits of Having a Trust:
- Protection of assets, while still maintaining control
- Plan in place for distribution of assets after death
- Tax advantage
- Helps avoid the process of probate

Types of Trusts

Revocable living trusts are the most common type of trust created. Although most are boilerplate documents tweaked to your needs, they can be quite dynamic and address a myriad of needs. You can, for example, modify your living trust to be an **incentive trust**. Let's say you have young children, and you die prematurely. Rather than allowing them to receive their entire inheritance at the age of eighteen, you can include a clause that stipulates money for college and then a match from the trust for whatever is earned through their job, up to a certain age. This can prevent the possibility of a child "spending it all" prematurely or simply becoming a "trust baby" who is not motivated to work.

There are also other types of estate planning trusts that have specific purposes. Here is a brief list of the more common ones and their uses:

Type of Trust	Purpose
Special Needs Trust (SNT)	Provides support for disabled loved ones
Asset Protection Trust (APT)	Reduces vulnerability to legal and other creditors
Dynastic or dynasty trust	Truly long-term succession
Charitable Remainder Trust (CRT)	Current income with a charitable bequest later

Type of Trust	Purpose
Spendthrift trust	Prevents heirs from direct access to funds
Qualified Terminable Interest Property Trust (QTIP)	Surviving spouse needs support before children inherit
Grantor Retained Annuity Trust (GRAT)	Grantor needs retirement income from assets
Generation-Skipping Trust (GST)	Avoids triggering generation-skipping tax for grandkids
Irrevocable Life Insurance Trust (ILIT)	Holds life insurance to pay estate tax or other liabilities
Crummey trust	Preserves lifetime gift tax exclusion
Irrevocable trust	Similar to a revocable living trust, but changes cannot be made without the approval of beneficiaries

Depending upon your family or business dynamics, your situation may warrant a different approach. Therefore, it is important to discuss this with a qualified advisor to help guide you in the right direction.

I cannot emphasize enough the importance of being specific regarding the instructions laid out in your trust. Many times, I have seen even the smallest ambiguity turn an estate plan into a disaster. Make sure your attorney has a clear understanding of your wishes and articulates them properly in the document. There are often "disgruntled" individuals (quite often family members) out there waiting to pounce and contest the deceased's trust. Because of this, I have often seen language in trusts that effectively disinherits any heir who contests an estate. Although this sounds harsh and perhaps unnecessary, adding such a clause has saved numerous families from unexpected legal battles and emotional trauma.

Choosing a Trustee

The job of a trustee can be a difficult one: emotional, challenging, and often unrewarding. Agreeing to accept this responsibility should not be taken lightly. It is a lot of work and liability even for someone who knows what they are doing, much less someone you have hastily selected, such as your oldest child or longtime friend. If there is any dissension in the family at all, it will likely manifest in distrust, jealousy, and all manner of problems for the sibling chosen, even though he or she has essentially taken on a part-time job as trustee. Although many people think it is best to have more than one trustee (for example, they cannot decide which of their two children to choose), this can often become a nightmare for several reasons. The kids may not agree with each other, or they may live in completely different geographical locations, which can cause significant delays when both signatures are required to move forward. For this and a host of other reasons, it is generally not advisable to set things up this way.

If you have an heir who has the potential to create an issue when your estate is settled, it is a good idea to not only address it in the estate plan but also to look to a **corporate trustee** or private fiduciary whose job it is to simply interpret the estate documents and carry out the plan. A corporate trustee, like a professional trust company, will be around much longer than you or your friends. If you have a child who has historically been plagued with dysfunction (unable to hold a job, with a history of substance abuse, or who has had issues with the law), a corporate trustee or private fiduciary is more resilient than your friend who may now be getting late-night phone calls or threats and may be bullied into releasing funds they are not supposed to release.

Traditionally, banks will offer to function as a type of corporate trustee to capture and control the way assets will be invested. They can be more difficult to work with, whereas a private corporate trustee or "advisor friendly" trustee may be a good choice, especially if you have a trusted advisor your family has been working with for an extended period. This is a fiduciary role, and as such, the corporate trustee's job is to ensure that it achieves the goals set by its creators. The trustee performs "non-discretionary" tasks, such as making income payments and preparing and filing taxes. "Discretionary" tasks give the trustee more room for interpretation. If the trust is silent on an issue, the trustee's fiduciary duty may require them to make discretionary decisions. For example, if a beneficiary makes a special demand for a distribution, the trustee may or may not decide to grant the request after considering the situation, documentation, sources of income, and other factors. In contrast, if a sibling (in the role of trustee) oversaw this decision, it might create, at the very least, an awkward situation.

The cost of utilizing a corporate trustee is typically determined by the value of the assets they are directing. Typically, these charges are 1 percent or less for administration and only begin once they have assumed the role of trustee after the final grantor or "owner-trustee" has died.

Moving Your Assets into the Trust

Imagine you decided to have a trust drawn up with your attorney. After some time and expense, you return home with a lovely binder containing your new legal documents. Congratulations! However, if you simply put your binder on the shelf, thinking, "That's that," your heirs would be in for a surprise one day. What is often overlooked by many after they decide to have a trust drafted is that the trust needs to *actually own* the assets for any of it to become effective. Therefore, you (or your attorney) need to go through the process of transferring your home, financial accounts, and so on into the trust as the new owner of the assets. This involves re-titling your home and financial accounts in the name of the trust. I have seen many situations over the years where people went through the process and expense of creating a trust only to have their estate go through probate (and the chaos that follows) because they never transferred assets into the trust!

If you have real estate, including a personal residence, you should get a current appraisal on each property, or at the very least, have your realtor run at least three "comps" for your property so you have a reasonable idea of the current value. If your heirs should decide to sell after your death, some, if not all, of that value will be "stepped-up" to fair market value at the time of death. This could make a significant difference in the case of rental property, as the depreciation taken each year is subtracted from the original value. If sold under ordinary circumstances, the owner would have to "recapture" all of that and the appreciation on the property, thus causing a much larger tax burden. However, at the time of death, with a "step-up," your heirs can either sell the property with no tax consequence or can, at the very least, erase all the depreciation taken to date and start over with the full fair market value should they keep and continue to rent and depreciate the property.

Reviewing Your Trust

Once you have your trust completed and assets transferred into it, pat yourself on the back! But because life constantly brings changes, you should have your trust reviewed about every three years to update because of changes in the law, tax code, and, most of all, in your life situation and assets. If it has been a long time since you have seen your attorney, or if he or she is no longer in business, you might need to seek out a new one. Chances are, your new attorney will tell you he or she wants to completely redo your trust. While this may sound like an expensive option, it is probably much cheaper than having him or her try to work with your old one. Why? Attorneys take on a lot of liability in the case that they miss something in someone else's extensive document.

Distributing Personal Possessions

You or your loved ones may have items of sentimental value to include in estate planning. The sooner you start the conversation with your parents about cleaning out the house, the better. Chances are they are overwhelmed with possessions collected over decades, which means you will likely be the one overwhelmed with their possessions one day. If there are items still dear to them that they are not ready to part with, and a family member expresses interest in it, this is a great time to include these with future distribution instructions in the estate plan (often done through a codicil in the will).

> *Rick's Story*
> *Prior to my brother's death and before my parents had developed a trust, they had a simple will in place in which my mom developed a plan for distributing their smaller personal possessions. As part of her planning, she spent weeks going throughout their home, placing blue or green painter's tape on the back of or under every item. I was not aware of this until my brother had died and I met with my parents about "what's next" in their end-of-life plan. At this point, my mom showed me all the personal items with the colored tape, indicating anything with blue tape would be mine, and anything with green would be for my brother. But then she said, "It doesn't matter now because everything belongs to you." Many emotion-filled conversations later led to my parents having a trust prepared. Little did I know that she would die just over one year later. Less than two years after her death, my dad was diagnosed with dementia, which meant all the planning we had accomplished was now taking effect. You never know what life will bring, so planning is a must!*

Arranging Guardianship

Along with a trustee, selecting a trusted guardian for minor children is another crucial element in estate planning. This is generally done through a will, which is the minimum you should have in place if you have minor children. Upon your death, while it may be assumed that a surviving spouse or sibling would take guardianship over your children, without a will in place, it is in the hands of the court to decide who that person should be. I cannot emphasize the importance of this enough. Something to note is that many people may not realize that if they establish a family living trust, a will is always part of that as well.

Picking a guardian to name in your will is no easy task. For example, my wife and I had a child later in life, and picking a guardian for our minor child while in our fifties was really challenging. In cases like this, parents are likely either gone or advanced in age, while siblings and friends have likely been down that road already and are not eager to parent all over again. Even younger couples often have a hard time deciding who should fill this role. Due to the difficulty of the decision, many people simply put it off. Sadly, I have been a witness to several situations that went badly as a result. Do not let this happen to your child. Choose wisely and make sure you have in-depth conversations with potential guardians to confirm they are the best choice for your family.

Establishing Powers of Attorney

Establishing a **Durable Power of Attorney** (DPOA) is an important step in your end-of-life planning. The assignment of a DPOA is typically part of drafting a will. It is important to note that it is a separate document that becomes part of the will and trust packet as a whole. Be sure to ask your attorney about the additional documents needed for assigning a DPOA when your will is being drafted. If you have an old will and trust, it is advisable to meet with your attorney to update your DPOA.

There are generally two categories that require designation of a DPOA: financial affairs and healthcare. A **financial DPOA** gives someone the power to act on your behalf to carry out the day-to-day operations of your financial life in the event you become incapacitated due to an illness, accident, or mental deficiency. Upon your death, this duty transfers to the trustee(s).

A **healthcare DPOA** names someone to represent your best interests and make health decisions for you in the event you are unable to. If you have selected different people for these tasks, it is a good idea to make sure that your financial DPOA and healthcare DPOA know each other and are both familiar with your situation and your wishes, as they will often need to work together if they are called to action. In either case, you are putting your finances or your life in the hands of another trusted individual. Choose someone who has your best interests at heart.

> *Rick's Story*
> *After Susie's death, I remarried, and now my wife, Lauren, is designated as my DPOA in our trust. When I had surgery several years ago, Lauren and I talked about my wishes if the surgery were to leave me incapacitated. I decided that I did not want to be on life-support but would rather be released to spend eternity with my Lord. My decision was also clearly articulated in our trust so there would be no mistakes. This is the benefit of planning for end-of-life: the confusion is removed, and the decision-making resides in the hands of the person affected.*

At-Need

Executing an Estate after the Death of a Loved One

If you have recently lost a loved one, you are likely overwhelmed with emotions, not knowing what to do next. My first advice is to take care of yourself, and if possible, find someone to help you through this time. That person could be a trusted friend or family member or even one of your advisors. Rick will talk more about building a support team in other chapters and in the Survivor Checklist© in the appendix. Even if you have all the answers printed here, the execution is still somewhat daunting under the circumstances. Please know that feeling overwhelmed is perfectly normal. Just to set expectations, even if an estate is simple and well-planned, you can still expect it to take six to eight months to settle, and as complexities grow, it is not uncommon for the process to take three years or longer.

What I (Kent) will attempt to do in the following pages is to give you a roadmap of things you or a team member should consider addressing. There are many administrative requirements that will need your attention, and many of them are extremely important decisions. They all come at a time when your cognitive skills may be slightly impaired due to the emotional trauma of loss (see chapter thirteen for more information on grieving). As an advisor, I find it most appropriate to hold off on making major decisions like selling a residence and perhaps moving to be closer to family. Decisions like this are life-altering, so remember to build a team of trusted friends and professionals for mentoring while on this journey.

The Will and Trust

Hopefully, the decedent had the foresight to have a will and trust drafted and you know where to find them (make sure you locate the signed copy). The attorney who drafted it will most likely have a copy, but in my experience, many people don't record the name of the attorney, who is often retired or even deceased when you reach out to him or her. The will and trust documents may be in a safety deposit box, which can be "frozen" at death and difficult to obtain. If you run into any of these issues, an advisor should be able to help you through this to obtain the documents.

If the decedent did have a will and trust and you are able to locate it, it is wise to seek the counsel of an attorney to determine proper distributions of assets or whether a probate needs to be opened. You will need to remove the name of the deceased from deeds and registrations on the accounts of capital assets like real estate and investments and then replace it with the name of the heir or trustee, if applicable. It is important to meet with an attorney at this time just to make sure everything is buttoned up in the estate documents.

Social Security and Annuities

The funeral home will usually report the death to the Social Security Administration (SSA), and you may be eligible for a one-time death benefit. Note that spouses must have been married for nine months or longer prior to death to qualify unless the death was the result of an accident or military service. Also, be aware that if your loved one had his or her Social Security checks directly deposited into a bank account, Social Security will take back the last direct deposit from the account at the time of death. While there are many things to understand about Social Security benefits, it is important to know that surviving spouses are eligible to receive the larger of either their own or their deceased spouse's payment for their lifetime, but with stipulations. Check with SSA for details regarding your specific situation. For more information on Social Security, see chapter twelve.

Annuities are tax-deferred retirement vehicles that can typically be rolled over to the surviving spouse or taken as income over time. If you have inherited an annuity, you are best served to contact a qualified financial advisor to help you determine the best course of action. You will need to contact the issuing institution to receive death claim paperwork. Often, there is more paperwork in the package than is required, so I recommend having someone you trust review it to make sure nothing is missed and so you don't spend time filling out unnecessary forms.

Stocks and Bonds

How an investment portfolio is registered makes a big difference in the taxation of appreciated securities at the death of a loved one. First, it is important to understand that capital assets like stocks, bonds, and real estate typically receive a "step-up" in value or "cost basis" at the time of death.

For example, if John Smith worked for XYZ Company all his life and participated in the stock purchase plan of that company with every paycheck for thirty years, chances are he has accumulated not only a lot of company stock, but it probably has had a substantial appreciation. Let us say that Mr. Smith put in

$50,000 of his own money over that time, but the stocks are worth $500,000 at his retirement. If he were to sell these at that time, he would recognize a capital gain of $450,000 and must pay taxes on that. If, however, he held it in a living trust and died, leaving it to his wife, the $50,000 he originally paid would be "stepped up" to the fair market value on the day of his death, thus giving his wife the opportunity to sell the entire $500,000 with no tax consequences. If he held it in his name only (not in a living trust), it would still receive a "step-up" but also would likely trigger probate. If at some point, Mr. Smith put it in both their names as "Joint Tenants with Rights of Survivorship," it would not necessarily trigger probate as it would automatically pass to the surviving spouse. But since it was not held in trust, only 50 percent of that original cost would be "stepped up," representing his (the deceased's) half of the assets. This would potentially create a tax burden if the surviving spouse chose to sell these assets for cash. If we are looking at highly appreciated real estate, this could make a huge difference in taxes to the surviving spouse. This is another good reason to consider a trust to hold your assets, and since rules vary between states, be sure to consult your tax, legal, and financial professional.

Another scenario I encounter all too often is that those same shares might be held in stock certificate form or even held in what is called a "clearing house" in a file cabinet somewhere, only to be discovered by heirs. This involves some effort to get the shares transferred into some form of brokerage account where they can be properly retitled and sold if desired. A share of stock in your file cabinet is not something you can do anything with until it is custodied by a brokerage firm. Further, to prove you are the heir, they will require you to supply a copy of the will or trust and several other forms to complete this process. Again, this is when you should ask for the help of either a trusted friend who knows how to navigate situations like this or a qualified financial professional.

After many years in this business, I have learned an important lesson: Unless your loved one was incredibly organized and you know where everything is, there is no substitute for digging through drawers and file cabinets to find necessary end-of-life documents. It is the rare occasion when I have seen someone who was so organized that everything was in its place and the heirs knew exactly where to look and what they were looking for. On one occasion just prior to the husband's passing, I was asked for help and located over $2 million in stock certificates in a disorganized file cabinet. I was able to help them get all of these squared away and into their newly-created trust just before he reached end-of-life. This is a rather extreme example, but without a system of organization, important documents can be elusive and require time and energy to locate.

Pensions and Company Benefits

Contact the decedent's former employer and ask them to send you a benefits summary, which may include life insurance, pension information, retirement plans, and more. If you were included as "joint and survivor" on your loved one's pension, you will need to submit paperwork for this to continue. Please be aware that there are several ways you can take a pension, and once chosen, the decision is irrevocable. The decedent may have signed up for his or her life only, which provided the highest monthly income but leaves nothing for his or her spouse once he or she has passed. If it was set up with a survivor benefit, it could be that you will receive the same amount as before or some lower percentage of that income, perhaps 75 percent or 50 percent.

In some cases, if you are the pensioner and your plan at the time had an option for a "pop-up provision," you would file paperwork showing that your spouse had pre-deceased you, and if this election were made, you would step back up to the income you would have had if you had elected your life only, resulting in additional monthly income. Either way, you will need to submit paperwork for this to continue.

In addition to pensions, there are often company benefits that remain even after retirement that one should be aware of. Pensions have what are called "survivorship options" for spouses of the deceased. If your spouse had a pension at the time of retirement, a decision had to be made either to take it for his or her life only or to provide for a surviving spouse at either 100 percent or some reduced percentage of what was being paid when both were alive. This is important for you to know.

Often, because there is a cost to the survivorship option, which reduces the monthly benefit amount, couples will opt to take the maximum amount only on the life of the pensioner to provide the greatest monthly cash flow. Or perhaps the pensioner was single at the time of retirement and so took the pension out on his or her life alone. Even if the pensioner marries, benefits will not continue to the surviving spouse after death since they married after the retirement selection was made.

If the deceased employee elected a 50 percent "joint and survivor option," the monthly amount going forward would be half of what they had been getting before. Some companies may provide a small life insurance policy or health insurance benefits that may change going forward for the surviving spouse. Again, these are things to discuss with the company's benefits department.

Other Things to Consider

As we have moved into the twenty-first century, many of the issues I have had to confront with survivors have taken on a new twist with the advent of the digital age. For example, I am often asked, "How do I access Mom's online bill pay at her bank?" or "How do I shut down my loved one's Facebook page or Amazon account?" These are just examples of the growing list of responsibilities that need to be addressed in an end-of-life situation. As lives become more complex, the list grows, and it is not possible to cover every scenario in the scope of this book. Suffice to say, it is usually wise to get some expert help.

> *A Note from Rick*
> *Throughout this chapter and book, I hope you take all this to heart and begin planning for your end-of-life and the incredible gift you can leave your family: an estate plan that eliminates chaos and allows heirs and others to mourn in a healthy*

way without the drama that occurs regularly. As a pastor, I have witnessed this often and have become a mediator for families just to develop a plan on how they will attend a funeral or memorial. Develop a plan and work the plan!

Action Steps

- If you don't already have a will or trust, make an appointment with an attorney who specializes in this area of law. Start by asking for recommendations from trusted family members or friends who have had a will or trust developed.
- If you already have a will and trust, make an appointment with your attorney to review your estate and make updates as necessary.
- If you have a family member with special needs, parents still living, or others who will have a financial or legal impact on you at their time of death, have a conversation with them about their estate planning.
- If you have minor children, start the discussion now about guardianship.

CHAPTER 3

Giving the Gift of Organ Donation

On the morning of April 24, 2007, at 2:30 a.m., my wife, Susie, began her new eternal life in heaven, leaving behind a valuable gift that I was not aware of—yet. I arrived home from the hospital around 6:00 in the morning and went to sleep, exhausted from being awake for nearly forty-eight hours as she progressively weakened. The phone rang at approximately 8:00 a.m., just a couple of hours after I went to bed. The person calling identified himself as a staff member with the agency for organ and tissue transplantation in Northern California.

"Your wife is registered as an organ and tissue donor," he said. "We have the opportunity to donate her organs to give the gift of sight to someone."

Still in a fog from a lack of sleep and sudden awakening—I asked, "Since she had more than thirty tumors in her bones (they quit counting after a scan was performed because there were so many), how can you take her corneas and transplant them?"

"Because the corneas are the only place in the body not affected by cancer. We can use them. May we proceed?"

I responded without hesitation because I knew this was important to her and me. "Yes, definitely, so someone can have sight!"

Years later, I contacted Donor Network West (donornetwork-west.org) to learn more about my late wife's gift. As it turned out, Susie's corneas were not used after all, but the fact that after all these years I was able to find current and verifiable information was impressive. Even though Susie's attempted organ donation was not successful, I still firmly believe in the value of making this gift beyond the grave.

The questions surrounding being a donor vary, but the commonality preventing someone from registering, I believe, is the lack of knowledge of both the need and process. Is that not true with most decision-making? We do not move forward because of inadequate knowledge, leaving us unsure and paralyzed at times. You can change this when it comes to making an informed decision about being an organ or tissue donor.

Beyond my personal experience through my wife's attempt as a donor, the information obtained for this chapter has come from conversations with the incredible people at Donor Network West, The American Association of Tissue Banks, and information available from various government websites.

Understanding the Donor Network Nationwide

There are fifty-seven federally designated organ procurement organizations (OPOs) nationwide. Each of these entities covers a given geographical area, allowing for a concentrated effort and efficiency. These entities can be found by state through the Health Resources & Services Administration's (HRSA) website www.organdonor.gov/awareness/organizations/local-opo.html.[1]

The lead donation and transplantation marketing entity, Donate Life America, hosts the National Donate Life Registry through RegisterMe.org.[2] This domain tracks approximately 4,000 registrations daily. Additionally, visitors and potential registrants have access to resources about being a donor, including patient stories and relevant factoids and infographics.

The American Association of Tissue Banks (AATB) is a professional, non-profit, scientific, and educational organization. AATB is the premier standard-setting body promoting the safety and use of donated human tissue. The association was founded in 1976 by a group of doctors and scientists who had started our nation's first tissue bank in 1949, the United States Navy Tissue Bank. The overwhelming majority of the human tissue distributed for transplant comes from AATB-accredited tissue banks. AATB supports the advancement of tissue-bank professionals and tissue-banking technologies, so no one suffers from the lack of donated human tissue. Learn more at https://www.aatb.org/.[3]

The process is simple to become an organ or tissue donor—it just takes some decision-making on your part.

The Basic Path of Donation

To assist you in understanding the steps of donation, I (Rick) have listed in chronological order the pathway to donation, how the process works, and the allocation methodology in the distribution of organs as a comprehensive blueprint for further study and implementation. The next step is up to you.

The following information has been taken directly from the U.S. Department of Health and Human Services website https://optn.transplant.hrsa.gov/learn/about-donation/the-basic-path-of-donation/.[4]

The donation process begins with a decision. You decide you want to help people with end-stage disease by donating your organs when you die. Your body, after all, is finished with them.

When your time comes, perhaps decades later, your organs may be used to save many lives. People most frequently become donors after a stroke, heart attack, or severe head injury.

Even though cases vary, the following describes the basic steps in donation from deceased donors.

Transport

A specialized team of EMTs and paramedics begin life-saving efforts at the scene. They also contact emergency-room doctors during transport.

Treatment

When the team arrives, ER doctors and nurses have advanced life-support equipment ready. They evaluate injuries and continue life-saving measures, including a ventilator, IV fluid, blood replacement, and drugs to help the heart keep beating.

Intensive Care

After vital signs stabilize, the patient is transferred to the ICU, where a doctor performs special tests to see how much damage has been done to the brain and organs. The medical team continues advanced life-support during the tests.

Brain Death Declared

Brain death is diagnosed as an irreversible loss of blood flow to the brain, causing the brain to die. After brain death, the donor's body is kept functioning by artificial means, such as ventilator support.

Evaluation

A specially-trained nurse from the organ procurement organization (OPO) goes to the hospital to see if the patient is medically suitable.

Consent

The doctor talks to the family about the patient's death. Then, someone from the OPO or specially-trained hospital staff talks to the family about donation. The family takes time to think and ask questions before they decide. The decision is easier if the patient is listed on the state donor registry and if the family had previously discussed donation.

Placement

The donor's blood type, height, weight, the hospital zip code, and other data are entered into the UNOS (United Network for Organ Sharing) national computer system to begin the organ allocation process. Appropriate candidates are found for whom the donor's organs are the best match. Timing is especially important at this step and during recovery.

Organ Recovery

The donor is taken to an operating room, where organs are surgically removed. After that, the organs are sent to the transplant hospitals, where candidates are waiting for them.

Funeral

After donation, the donor is taken to a funeral home, and the OPO works with the funeral director to avoid delays in the funeral. Because organ donation is rarely disfiguring, the family can have an open casket.

Follow-up

A few weeks later, the OPO sends a letter to the donor's family, telling them which organs were transplanted but keeping the names of the recipients confidential. Most OPOs continue to provide support to donor families, such as bereavement counseling and, later, memorial events.

How Organ Allocation Works

The following information has been taken directly from the U.S. Department of Health and Human Services website https://optn.transplant.hrsa.gov/learn/about-transplantation/ how-organ-allocation-works/.[5]

More than 120,000 people in the US are waiting to receive a life-giving organ transplant. We simply don't have enough donated organs to transplant to everyone in need, so we balance factors of:

- Justice (fair consideration of candidates' circumstances and medical needs).
- Medical utility (trying to increase the number of transplants performed and the length of time patients and organs survive).

Many factors used to match organs with patients in need are the same for all organs, but the system must accommodate some unique differences for each organ.

The First Step

Before an organ is allocated, all transplant candidates on the waiting list who are incompatible with the donor because of blood type, height, weight, and other medical factors are automatically screened from any potential matches. Then, the computer application determines the order that the other candidates will receive offers, according to national policies.

Geography Plays a Part

There are fifty-seven local donation service areas and eleven regions that are used for US organ allocation. Hearts and lungs have less time to be transplanted, so we use a radius from the donor hospital instead of regions when allocating those organs.

The Right-Sized Organ

Proper organ size is critical to a successful transplant, which means that children often respond better to child-sized organs. Although pediatric candidates have their own unique scoring system, children essentially are first in line for other children's organs.

Factors in Organ Allocation

Blood type and other medical factors weigh into the allocation of every donated organ, but other factors are unique to each organ type.

Kidney
- Waiting time
- Donor/recipient immune system incompatibility
- Pediatric status
- Prior living donor
- How far from donor hospital
- Survival benefit (starting in 2015)

Heart
- Medical need
- How far from donor hospital

Lung
- Survival benefit
- Medical urgency
- Waiting time
- Distance from donor hospital

Liver
- Medical need
- Distance from donor hospital

Preserving Organs

Donated organs require special methods of preservation to keep them viable between the time of procurement and transplantation.

Common maximum organ preservation times
- Heart, lung: 4–6 hours
- Liver: 8–12 hours
- Pancreas: 12–18 hours
- Kidney: 24–36 hours

Donor Matching System

The following information has been taken from the U.S. Department of Health and Human Services website https:// optn.transplant.hrsa.gov/learn/about-transplantation/ donor-matching-system/.[6]

When transplant hospitals accept patients onto the waiting list, the patients are registered in a centralized, national computer network that links all donors and transplant candidates. The UNOS Organ Center is staffed twenty-four hours a day throughout the year, and it assists with the matching, sharing, and transportation of organs via this computer network.

Transplant centers, tissue-typing laboratories, and OPOs are involved in the organ sharing process. When donor organs are identified, the procuring organization typically accesses the computerized organ matching system, enters information about the donor organs, and runs the match program. At times, when requested or when there is a need to identify perfectly matched kidney donors/ recipients, the matching process is handled by organ center personnel at UNOS headquarters in Richmond, Virginia.

For each organ that becomes available, the computer program generates a list of potential recipients ranked according to objective criteria (i.e., blood type, tissue type, size of the organ, medical urgency of the patient, time on the waiting list, and distance between donor and recipient). Each organ has its own specific criteria. Ethnicity, gender, religion, and financial status are not part of the computer matching system.

After printing the list of potential recipients, the procurement coordinator contacts the transplant surgeon caring for the top-ranked patient (i.e., the patient whose organ characteristics best match the donor organ and whose time on the waiting list, urgency status, and distance from the donor organ adhere to allocation policy) to offer the organ. Depending on various factors, such as the donor's medical history and the current health of the potential recipient, the transplant surgeon determines if the organ is suitable for the patient. If the organ is turned down, the next listed individual's transplant center is contacted, and so on, until the organ is placed.

Once the organ is accepted for a potential recipient, transportation arrangements are made for the surgical teams to come to the donor hospital, and surgery is scheduled. For heart, lung, or liver transplantation, the recipient of the organ is identified prior to the organ recovery and called into the hospital, where the transplant will occur to prepare for the surgery.

The recovered organs are stored in a cold organ preservation solution and transported from the donor to the recipient hospital. For heart and lung recipients, it is best to transplant the organ within six hours of organ recovery. Livers can be preserved up to twenty-four hours after recovery. For kidneys and typically the pancreas, laboratory tests designed to measure the compatibility between the donor organ and recipient are performed. A surgeon will not accept the organ if these tests show that the patient's immune system will reject the organ. Therefore, the recipient is usually not identified until after these organs are recovered.

The role of the organ procurement organization (OPO) is very important in the matching process. OPOs become involved when a patient is identified as a potential donor. The OPO coordinates the logistics between the organ donor's family, donor organs, transplant center(s), and potential transplant candidate.

OPOs provide organ recovery services to hospitals located within designated geographical areas of the US. OPOs are non-profit organizations and, like transplant hospitals, are members of the Organ Procurement Transplantation Network (OPTN). Each has its own board of directors and a medical director on staff who is usually a transplant surgeon or physician.

OPOs employ highly trained professionals called procurement coordinators, who carry out the organization's mission. Once contacted by the hospital with a potential donor, OPO staff:

- Conduct a thorough medical and social history of the potential donor to help determine the suitability of organs for transplantation.
- Work with hospital staff to offer the option of donation to the donor family.
- Ensure that the decision to donate is based on informed consent.

- Manage the clinical care of the donor once consent for donation is finalized.
- Enter the donor information into the UNOS computer to find a match for the donated organs.
- Coordinate the organ recovery process with the surgical teams and provide follow-up information to the donor family and involved hospital staff regarding the outcome of the donations.

From the moment of consent for donation to the release of the donor's body to the morgue, all costs associated with the organ donation process are billed directly to the OPO.

OPOs also promote organ donation in their community by sponsoring workshops on organ donation and participating in community health fairs and events. OPO hospital development coordinators also work with hospitals to help educate the staff on the donation process and care of the donor family. To find out about the OPO in your area, go to https://optn.transplant.hrsa.gov/members/member-directory/.[7]

Organ Donation Myths and Facts

Sometimes, myths and misperceptions about organ, eye, and tissue donation can prevent someone from signing up. Imagine the lives we could save if everyone knew the true facts about donation. You can help bust the myths about organ donation—and help save lives—by learning and sharing these facts. *The following information has been adapted from https://www.organdonor.gov/learn/faq.*[8]

Myth: I have a medical condition, so I can't be a donor.
Fact: Anyone, regardless of age or medical history, can sign up to be a donor. The transplant team will determine at an individual's time of death whether donation is possible. Even with an illness, you may be able to donate your organs or tissues.

Myth: I'm too old to be a donor.

Fact: There's no age limit to organ donation. To date, the oldest donor in the US was age ninety-three. What matters is the health and condition of your organs when you die.

Myth: If they see I'm a donor at the hospital, they won't try to save my life.

Fact: When you are sick or injured and admitted to a hospital, the one and only priority is to save your life. Period. Donation doesn't become a possibility until all lifesaving methods have failed.

Myth: Rich or famous people on the waiting list get organs faster.

Fact: A national computer system matches donated organs to recipients. The factors used in matching include blood type, time spent waiting, other important medical information, how sick the person is, and geographic location. Race, income, and celebrity are never considered.

Myth: My family won't be able to have an open-casket funeral if I'm a donor.

Fact: An open casket funeral is usually possible for organ, eye, and tissue donors. Through the entire donation process, the body is treated with care, respect, and dignity.

Myth: My family will have to pay for the donation.

Fact: There is no cost to donors or their families for organ or tissue donation.

Myth: Somebody could take my organs and sell them.

Fact: Federal law prohibits buying and selling organs in the US. Violators can be punished with prison sentences and fines.

Myth: If I'm in a coma, they could take my organs.
Fact: The majority of deceased organ donors are patients who have been declared brain dead. But brain death is not the same as a coma. People can recover from comas but not from brain death. Brain death is final.

Myth: People in the LGBTQ community can't donate.
Fact: There is no policy or federal regulation that excludes a member of the LGBTQ community from donating organs. What matters in donating organs is the health of the organs.

Faith and Science

Most major religions in the United States support organ donation and consider organ donation as the final act of love and generosity toward others.

Each decision to become a donor is a personal one. We suggest consulting with your faith leader if you have questions about your religion and donation. Below, you'll find official statements or policies about how some religions and denominations in the US view donation. These statements are quoted by permission from the Donate Life website.[9]

Amish

The Amish will consent to transplantation if they believe it is for the well-being of the transplant recipient. John Hostetler, world-renowned authority on Amish religion and professor of anthropology at Temple University in Philadelphia, says in his book *Amish Society*, "The Amish believe that since God created the human body, it is God who heals. However, nothing in the Amish understanding of the Bible forbids them from using modern medical services, including surgery, hospitalization, dental work, anesthesia, blood transfusions, or immunization."[10]

Assembly of God

The decision to donate is left up to the individual. Donation is highly supported by the denomination.[11]

Baptist

Though Baptists generally believe that organ and tissue donation and transplantation are ultimately matters of personal conscience, the nation's largest Protestant denomination, the Southern Baptist Convention, adopted a resolution in 1988, encouraging physicians to request organ donation in appropriate circumstances and to ". . . encourage voluntarism regarding organ donations in the spirit of stewardship, compassion for the needs of others, and alleviating suffering." Other Baptist groups have supported organ and tissue donation as an act of charity and leave the decision to donate up to the individual.[12]

Buddhism

Organ and tissue donation is considered an individual's decision. Buddhism does not promote or prohibit donation, but if an individual decides to become an organ donor, it is widely lauded as an act of compassion. In the case of deceased donation, the death process is an important, highly respected time for Buddhists, and the requests of the deceased take precedence.[13]

Catholicism

Organ, eye, and tissue donation is an acceptable act of kindness in the Roman Catholic Church. Donation is considered an act of charity and love, according to Pope John Paul II in Evangelium Vitae, no. 86.[14]

Christian Science

The Church of Christ Scientist does not have a specific position regarding organ donation. According to the First Church of Christ Scientist in Boston, Christian Scientists normally rely on spiritual instead of medical means of healing. They are free, however, to choose whatever form of medical treatment they desire—including a transplant. The question of organ and tissue donation is an individual decision.[15]

Disciples of Christ

Organ and tissue donation is accepted and actively promoted by the Christian church. In 1985, the General Assembly adopted "Resolution #8548 Concerning Organ Transplants," which encouraged members to register as organ donors and support transplant recipients through prayer.[16]

Episcopal

Organ donation is encouraged by the Episcopal Church. The 70th General Convention adopted "Resolution #1991–A097 Urge Members to Consider Donating Organs," which recommended that members donate their organs after death so that others may live. The church also urges members to clearly state their decision to family, friends, the church, and their attorney.[17]

Evangelical Covenant Church

Organ donation is acceptable and encouraged by the Evangelical Covenant Church. Since the adoption of the Organ Donor Resolution in 1982, members of the church are encouraged to register their decision to be a donor. Leaders of the faith, especially educators, are encouraged to promote awareness of organ donation in all evangelical congregations.[18]

Greek Orthodox

According to Reverend Dr. Milton Efthimiou, director of the Department of Church and Society for the Greek Orthodox Church of North and South America, "The Greek Orthodox Church is not opposed to organ donation as long as the organs and tissue in questions are used to better human life, i.e., for transplantation or for research that will lead to improvements in the treatment and prevention of disease."[19]

Hinduism

Organ donation is not prohibited by religious law, according to the Hindu Temple Society of North America. Donation is considered an individual's decision. There are many references that support organ donation in Hindu scriptures. *Daan* is the original word in Sanskrit for donation, meaning selfless giving. It is also third in the list of the ten *Niyamas* (virtuous acts). Life after death is a strong belief of Hindus and is an ongoing process of rebirth.[20]

Islam

In 2019, the Fiqh Council of North America (FCNA) announced that organ donation and transplantation is permissible within the Islamic faith and among American Muslims, making a clear religious ruling for Muslims living in North America. Organ donation is permitted in the Islamic faith as long as shar'i guidelines are met and measures are in place to protect human dignity. Living donation is permitted to keep the recipient alive or an essential function of their body intact. In the case of deceased donation, permission must be given by the deceased before his or her death or by his or her heirs after death.[21]

Judaism

Organ, eye, and tissue donation is encouraged in the Jewish faith. Donation and transplantation does not desecrate a body or show lack of respect for the dead, and any delay in burial to facilitate organ donation is respectful of the decedent. Organ donation saves lives and honors the deceased. The Conservative Movement's Committee on Jewish Laws and Standards has stated that organ donations after death represent not only an act of kindness but are also a "commanded obligation" that saves human lives.[22]

Lutheran Church

Organ donation is permitted and encouraged in the Lutheran Church. In the Church's 1984 resolution, "Organ Donation: A Resolution of the Lutheran Church in America," it is stated that donation contributes to the well-being of humanity and is an expression of love for a neighbor in need. The Lutheran Church encourages members to make the necessary family legal arrangements, including registering as a donor.[23]

Mennonite

Mennonites have no formal position on donation but are not opposed to it. They believe the decision to donate is up to the individual or their family.[24]

(Mormon) Church of Jesus Christ of Latter-day Saints

Organ and tissue donation is permitted by the Church of Jesus Christ of Latter-day Saints. Donation is considered a selfless act with great medical benefit to recipients. The decision to donate organs or other tissue rests with the individual or deceased donor's family.[25]

Presbyterian

Organ donation is encouraged by the Presbyterian Church, but the ability to donate is up to the individual and what he or she wants to do with his or her body. The Presbyterian Church (USA) encouraged all Christians to become organ and tissue donors in their 1983 General Assembly as an act of ministry to others.[26]

Sikh

The Sikh philosophy and teachings support the importance of giving and putting others before oneself. Seva (the act of selfless service, to give without seeking reward or recognition) is at the core of being a Sikh. Seva can also be about donating your organ to another—Sikhism does not attach taboos to organ donation and transplantation and stresses that saving a human life is one of the noblest things you can do. Sikhs also believe that your body does not need all its organs at or after death.[27]

Southern Baptist Convention

Organ donation is considered an act of stewardship and com-passion that alleviates the suffering of others by the Southern Baptist Convention. In their 1988 resolution, "Resolution on Human Organ Donations," the convention determined that resur-rection does not depend on body wholeness.[28]

United Methodist

Organ and tissue donation is encouraged by the United Methodist Church. In their 2000 resolution, "Resolution #139," the church promoted the celebration of National Donor Sabbath as another way that its members can help save lives.[29]

Action Steps

- Have a conversation with family members about registering to be a tissue or organ donor.
- If you need additional input from your house of worship, medical professionals, a donor organization in your area, or family members, take the next step and set a time to discuss this opportunity to give a gift.
- If you have made the decision to be a donor, then go to the government website that will help you find your individual state and sign up online at www.donatelifeamerica.net.

CHAPTER 4

Receiving Hospice Care

Caring for the sick and disabled is not new; in fact, it is part of who we are as human beings. The desire to help others has been built into our DNA, and our compassion as a species extends beyond family members and friends. When you consider the funds and manpower focused on meeting the needs of others on a global basis, whether through government programs, private firms, non-profits, faith-based hospitals, or individual caregivers, it is immeasurable. You cannot put a dollar value on it. A matrix does not exist to measure something that is done daily in homes, communities, and nations through the loving hearts of people who care. All we can really do is marvel at the care given and the people providing it.

As with every part of this book, my goal is to make you aware of an end-of-life topic, offer information to help guide you through the process, and then leave you with encouragement to do your homework. Doing your own work means you will learn more and have firsthand information as a result. This chapter is no different. Information on hospice is easily found online, although it can be complex and difficult to understand while maneuvering through government regulations. To help narrow the scope of this chapter, I've organized it by the chronological order of events that will occur when seeking hospice care. My co-author on this topic is Rena Robinson, a registered nurse (RN) and the director of community relations for a hospice provider. Rena has more experience with hospice care than anyone I know. Through her contribution, you'll gain more insight into hospice care, how this amazing industry operates, and their incredible servant hearts to do what they do.

The History of Hospice Care

Hospice care, like every organization or movement, has a beginning, but you may be surprised to learn just how old and new it is. History is debatable on the source of hospice care, but there is agreement to its possible origin dating back to the fourth century, when monasteries and other religious faiths provided care to the elderly, sick, and travelers—who were primarily indigent. Care systems advanced in Europe in the eleventh century, and by the mid-1800s, England had developed a formalized system, which culminated in the first "modern hospice" in 1967. The United States followed with its first modern-day hospice care in the early 1970s, and since its inception, hospice care organizations' appearance and methodology have evolved into a highly functioning source of personal care.

What had started out as a volunteer-led movement to improve care for people ultimately became—for the United States—a Congress-created Medicare hospice benefit in the early 1980s. In 1993, hospice became a guaranteed benefit in the United States and a significant part of health care.[1] Receiving care at home, nursing homes, assisted living facilities, veteran's facilities, and prisons reduced Medicare costs by minimizing emergency room and in-hospital patient visits. Because hospice is covered under the Medicare hospice benefit and is guaranteed under the Medicare system in the US, pre-need planners should become familiar with this benefit.

The Difference between Hospice and Palliative Care

Hospice and palliative care are not the same. Palliative care's focus is on pain and symptom management while working toward curative treatment. Hospice is focused on end-of-life care after treatment options have been exhausted or declined. Palliative care can precede hospice, does not have time restrictions, and does not require a terminal diagnosis.

While hospice is a Medicare-sponsored source of care, palliative care does not share the identical benefit. Palliative care is often provided through your physician in conjunction with nurse practitioners, social workers, and chaplaincy services acting as coordinators. Your medical provider may also include specialists, such as speech and physical therapists, dieticians, and pharmacists (check for co-pays and limitations within your plan). Depending upon your individual plan, Medicare Part B and Medicaid—if you qualify—does provide coverage, but there may be co-pays and limitations.

The Hospice Care Process

(Rena) Navigating uncharted waters can be a frightening experience for any of us—especially when trying to understand rules and regulations while experiencing end-of-life. Having someone assist you who is experienced in both federal and state Medicare/Medicaid law can help ease this process because of the complexity of regulations surrounding this benefit. Although you may feel overwhelmed now, you are not alone. You and the hospice team you choose are on this journey together.

Qualifying for Hospice Care

Qualifying for hospice care usually begins with a referral from your physician. Based on your current terminal or life-limiting condition(s) and your trajectory of decline, your physician is anticipating that you will have fewer than six months to live. You will need a physician's order for a hospice evaluation. Your physician or provider will give this order to the hospice provider you choose.

Once you are under hospice care, the hospice team is required by law to review your individualized plan of care every two weeks to determine if you still meet hospice eligibility guidelines. Based on your individual hospice terminal diagnosis, if you continue showing improvement or "stabilization," you may be discharged from hospice care due to an extended prognosis. You do have the right to appeal the discharge upon this decision, and you may be allowed to stay on after appeal review.

Choosing a Hospice Care Provider

Your hospice provider of choice will help you navigate these uncharted waters together; this is what we do. Seeking and securing a qualified hospice representative to guide you through the recommendations and decision-making can be your best ally. Once the patient and hospice representative have concluded the initial process, a case manager—who is an RN—is assigned to complete the paperwork and remains the contact person for administrative assistance. As a patient, you and your family are probably unfamiliar with the system, and the guidance of a qualified case manager can eliminate mistakes and regulation oversights, making sure you receive the full benefit of the program.

The following sections contain information adapted by permission from the CaringInfo website, a program of the National Hospice and Palliative Care Organization (NHPCO), at https://www.caringinfo.org/types-of-care/hospice-care/choosing-and-finding-hospice-care/.[2]

Accreditation

Misconceptions arise from a lack of knowledge and investigation. One misconception I (Rick) had years ago was that hospice was *one* organization serving the entire country. Not true. There are numerous hospice providers—well over 4,300 nationwide as of 2016—throughout the country that share a common goal: care for the ill. But their services vary depending upon the need and the number of hospice providers in your given area. So how are these different hospice providers governed? Many hospice providers apply for *accreditation* and are approved through organizations where guidelines have been established and governance adhered to, in addition to state laws. When interviewing a hospice provider of your choice, inquire about their accreditation to see if they are in good standing and through what organization. If a hospice provider is not accredited through a national organization, then outside of state laws, what governance do they submit to?

Other questions to ask when researching a hospice provider include:

- *Is the hospice Medicare-certified?* Most hospices are certified by Medicare and are therefore required to follow Medicare rules and regulations. This is important if you wish to receive hospice care as part of your Medicare/Medicaid coverage.

- *Has the hospice been surveyed by a state or federal oversight agency in the last five years?* Ask when the last survey was and if any deficiencies were noted, and if so, have they been resolved.

- *Is the hospice accredited by a national organization?* Several organizations accredit hospices, surveying them to ensure they meet quality standards. Hospices are not required to be accredited, but accreditation can reflect their commitment to quality.

- *Does the hospice conduct a family evaluation survey?* Many hospices ask family members to complete a brief evaluation of their services after the death of a loved one. Ask for their most recent scores so you can see how previous patients and family members have rated their services.

- *Are clinical staff (physicians, advanced practice nurses, nurses, nursing assistants, social workers, and chaplains) certified or credentialed in hospice and palliative care?* There are several credentials that hospice professionals can achieve based on their knowledge of hospice/palliative care and their educational experience.

59

Levels of Care

There are four types of hospice care:
1. Routine Home Care
2. Continuous Home Care
3. General Inpatient Care
4. Respite Care

Each hospice organization in the country is required to provide all levels of care, but each provider may use different terms, define them differently, and excel in one area but maybe not in another. Therefore, when you begin your research for your given area, go online and examine what terminology they use and the exact description of that level of service. Each hospice should provide some level of care in each level.

Questions to Ask

Depending on where you live, there could be one or several hospice providers serving your community. If there are multiple hospice providers in your area, you can decide—through research—which provider can serve you best. Then set up a time to speak to their hospice representative for more information and details specific to their hospice agency. When you speak to the hospice representative about the services provided, ask these questions to help guide your decision-making.
- What services are provided?
- What kind of support is available to the family/caregiver?
- What roles do the attending physician and hospice play?
- What does the hospice volunteer do?
- How does hospice work to keep the patient comfortable?
- How are services provided after hours?
- How and where does hospice provide short-term inpatient care?
- With which nursing homes or long-term care facilities does the hospice work?

- Does the hospice own or operate a care facility to provide home-like care in a hospice residence, hospital, or nursing home?
- How long does it typically take the hospice to enroll someone once the request for services is made?

All hospices provide expert medical care, emotional and spiritual care, medicines, medical supplies and equipment, volunteers, and grief support after the death of a loved one. In addition to these services, some hospices offer specialized programs for children, people with specific diseases, "pre-hospice" care for individuals not yet medically ready for hospice care, and other "extra" services that may benefit your family. Some hospice programs also offer therapy, such as physical, occupational, respiratory, music, pet, and massage therapy.

Once you choose a hospice provider, you can later transfer to a different hospice provider if you are unhappy with your choice. However, you may transfer to another hospice provider only one time during each election period. You may also revoke hospice services at any time should you decide to pursue alternative curative treatment or change your mind.

For additional frequently asked questions about hospice, visit the CaringInfo website at https://www.caringinfo.org/?s=frequently+asked+questions.

Establishing Your Hospice Team

The following information is quoted by permission from the CaringInfo website, a program of the National Hospice and Palliative Care Organization (NHPCO), at https://www.caringinfo.org/types-of-care/hospice-care/.[3]

Hospice care is a person and family-centered approach that includes, at a minimum, a team of doctors, nurses, home health aides, social workers, chaplains, counselors, and trained volunteers. They work together focusing on the patient's needs, whether physical, emotional, or spiritual. The goal is to help keep the patient as pain-free as possible with loved ones nearby. The hospice team develops a care plan that meets each person's individual needs for pain management and symptom control (you or your designated decision-maker have the right to continue participating in the development of your ongoing plan of care).

The team usually consists of:

- Clergy or other counselors.
- Home health aides.
- Hospice physician (or medical director).
- Nurses.
- Social workers.
- Trained volunteers.
- Speech, physical, and occupational therapists, if needed.
- The person's personal physician may also be included.

It is important to find out what the role of the patient's primary doctor will be once the patient begins receiving hospice care. Most often, a person can choose to have his or her personal doctor involved in the medical care. Both the physician and hospice medical director may work together to coordinate the patient's medical care, especially when symptoms are difficult to manage. Regardless, a physician's involvement is important to ensure quality hospice care. The hospice medical director is also available to answer questions the patient or loved ones may have regarding hospice medical care.

In many cases, family members or loved ones are the patient's primary caregivers. As a relationship with the hospice provider begins, hospice staff will want to know how best to support the person and family during this time.

Among its major responsibilities, the interdisciplinary hospice team:

- Manages the patient's pain and symptoms.
- Provides emotional support.
- Provides needed medications, medical supplies, and equipment.
- Coaches loved ones on how to care for the patient.
- Delivers special services like speech and physical therapy when needed.

- Makes short-term inpatient care available when pain or symptoms become too difficult to manage at home or the caregiver needs respite time.
- Provides grief support to surviving loved ones and friends. Support can include conversations with the person and family members, teaching caregiving skills, prayer, telephone calls to loved ones, including family members who live at a distance, and companionship and help from volunteers.

Counseling or grief support for the patient and loved ones is an important part of hospice care. After the person's death, bereavement support is offered to families for at least one year. These services can take a variety of forms, including telephone calls, visits, written materials about grieving, and support groups. Individual counseling may be offered by the hospice provider, or they may make a referral to a community resource.

> *Locating Your Local Hospice/Palliative Care Organization*
> To find a hospice in your community, go to https://www.nhpco.org/find-a-care-provider or call National Hospice and Palliative Care Organization's Help Line: 800-568-8898 or 703-837-1500.

Starting Care

The following information is quoted by permission from the CaringInfo website, a program of the National Hospice and Palliative Care Organization (NHPCO), at https://www.caringinfo.org/types-of-care/hospice-care/choosing-and-finding-hospice-care/.[4]

Anyone can inquire about hospice services. You or your loved one may call a local hospice and request services. The hospice staff will then contact your physician to determine if a referral to hospice is appropriate. Another way to inquire about hospice is to talk with your physician, and he or she can make a referral to hospice.

Usually, care is ready to begin within a day or two of referral. However, in urgent situations, service may begin sooner. Hospice can begin as soon as the hospice nurse visits to make sure you meet hospice guidelines. The hospice nurse will also review the services the hospice will offer and sign the necessary consent forms for care to begin.

> *A Note from Rick*
> *My conversations with Rena revealed a different reality than the opinion above, stating that care can begin within a day or two of referral. Although it is possible, that is not normal. Quite often, a referral can take multiple days waiting for a physician to complete the process, so the patient must wait for hospice care. Additionally, the lack of a designated decision-maker for a patient unable to comprehend complex issues or sign for him or herself will delay the process. Written consents must be signed before care begins. One way to approach this for a timelier process is to help your hospice case manager by calling the physician yourself and requesting that he or she expedite the process. It may take more than one call, but persistence pays off. Also, make every effort to have consents signed at your earliest opportunity since care will not begin until this is completed.*

Paying for Hospice Care

If you have healthcare through Medicare, hospice benefits are covered 100 percent as it relates to your terminal diagnosis and in conjunction with your individualized hospice plan of care. Your hospice representative can explain this more fully. Hospice benefits should cover medications and "durable medical equipment"

(DME) like a hospital bed, wheelchair, shower chair, oxygen, and so on, but each patient's care is individualized based on his or her terminal diagnosis. Your hospice representative can help explain the uniqueness of your care and what equipment is covered.

Verify with your hospice case manager the distinction between certification periods. The Medicare hospice benefit consists of two ninety-day benefit periods and an unlimited number of sixty-day benefit periods (a patient must continue to meet eligibility criteria). Simply not understanding these two distinctly different applications of hospice could limit your use or cost you money out-of-pocket. For more information, go to Medicare.gov.

If you are not eligible for Medicare, check with your health insurance provider to find out if they cover hospice care and what those benefits include.

Dispelling Myths about Hospice Care

The following information has been quoted by permission from VeryWell Health's website https://www.verywellhealth.com/hospice-care-4014065.[5]

Despite continual growth in awareness and access, society still harbors many myths about hospice and the care it provides. These misconceptions contribute to the underutilization of hospice services. This is unfortunate because many patients with life-limiting illnesses could benefit from expert pain and symptom control and the emotional, social, and spiritual support that hospice care can provide. Learn the truth behind four common hospice myths that contribute to the stigma surrounding this form of end-of-life care.

Myth #1: Hospice Care Means Giving Up Hope

Many people mistakenly believe that patients who choose to enter hospice have given up hope, but the truth is that those facing a life-limiting illness or terminal disease have chosen to redefine their hopes. Where a patient once hoped for a cure, he or she might now hope to live pain-free. For other hospice patients, hope might mean seeing a distant friend or relative one last time or taking a trip to the beach. For still others, hope could be as simple as wanting to spend as much time with loved ones as possible or remaining at home rather than going to the hospital or a nursing home.

Hope looks different in hospice care, but it is certainly not lost. A hospice caregiving team can help patients accomplish tasks, fulfill wishes, and maintain hope during their remaining time.

Myth #2: Hospice Means I Must Sign a DNR

A do-not-resuscitate (DNR) order is one of the several legal documents people use when establishing their advance healthcare directive. A DNR means that you do not want to be resuscitated via cardiopulmonary resuscitation (CPR) or other means should your breathing cease or your heart stop beating.

Signing a DNR is not a requirement to receive hospice care. While many hospice patients elect to have a DNR in place, a DNR is not the right choice for everyone. The goal of hospice is patient comfort with the *patient* directing his or her care. No decisions should ever be forced upon patients, including those in hospice.

Myth #3: Hospice Is Only for Cancer Patients

As of 2017, 74 percent of patients were admitted to hospice with non-cancer primary diagnoses, with only 26 percent having cancer as their primary diagnosis. Some of the most common non-cancer diagnoses in a hospice in 2017 were heart disease, dementia, lung disease, and stroke or coma. While hospice case manager nurses and other caregiving professionals are very skilled at managing the symptoms of cancer, they are equally skilled at managing the symptoms of many other forms of chronic illness.

Myth #4: Hospice Is Only for Patients Actively Dying or Close to Death

In 2017, the median length of service for hospice patients was twenty-four days. This means that of the estimated 1.5 million patients who received hospice services that year, half received hospice care for less than twenty-four days, and the other half received it for longer than that. In fact, the average number of days a patient received hospice care in 2017 was 76.1 days.

The dying process takes time. Because of the highly skilled care that hospice workers can provide to their patients, hospice proves most effective when the caregiving team has time to deliver it. Patients and their loved ones need support, information, and medical care. Social workers and chaplains need time to work with patients and their families to bring them to a place of acceptance. Nurses and doctors need time to optimally manage the patient's symptoms.

Now is the best time to learn more about hospice care and ask questions about what to expect. Although end-of-life care may be difficult to discuss, it is best for loved ones and family members to share their wishes long before it becomes a concern. This can greatly reduce stress when the time for hospice becomes apparent. By having these discussions in advance, uncomfortable situations can be avoided. Instead, educated decisions can be made that include the advice and input of loved ones.

Action Steps

- Contact friends and family who have experience with hospice care providers for their input.
- If you have Medicare or Medicaid, learn how to apply/qualify for hospice care.
- Have a discussion with your loved ones about your desires should you choose hospice care.
- Discuss with your family and doctor who will help make the decision to start hospice care. Decide who will be the primary caregiver and then establish a schedule involving other family members or friends willing to help.

CHAPTER 5

Struggling with Sudden Death

I received a call in the early morning on May 1, 2017, that my dad's vitals were dropping quickly. He was in the hospital, having suffered a stroke the day before. The nurse said over the phone, "You better come quick."

Within twenty minutes, I was at the hospital. When I arrived, the nurse was removing the wires and tubes from his body. "He just passed away before you walked in. I'm sorry, Mr. Craig, your dad is gone."

He was ninety-one years old and my hero. After the shock of realizing he was gone, I put my hand on his chest, spoke to him, and thanked him for being such an incredible father. Then I asked the nurse, "How long do I have before I have to move him to a funeral home?"

The nurse looked me in the eye and without hesitation said, "You have six hours, but you've already been here for about thirty minutes, so you have five-and-a-half hours because we don't have a morgue."

Devastated, angry, and confused would be a mild way of describing how I felt. Why had they not told me this the day before when he first arrived at the emergency department and was diagnosed with a life-threatening stroke? Without the luxury of time, I was faced (once again) with decisions that had to be made immediately.

There is little in life that could be more of a shock than getting that call or knock on the door and learning that a loved one has died. Notification can come from your doctor, law enforcement, chaplain, military personnel, employer, family, friend, or sometimes even social media. Regardless of the means of notification, it can be debilitating if not paralyzing to the recipient of the news. No one knows that better than my friend Phil Handley, a former paramedic, retired Napa Fire Department captain, and volunteer chaplain for the Napa PD, Sheriff's Department, and Fire Department. After four years in the US Coast Guard involving numerous rescues and recoveries, Phil discovered his calling: helping others. He lived out that calling during his thirty-five years of service as a first responder, where he was on-scene for countless fatalities and was often the one to inform surviving family members of the death. In each encounter with a surviving family member or friend, Phil poured out grace, love, professionalism, and total devotion to his job.

With Phil's extensive training in rescue and recovery, I asked him to walk us through the protocol as a first responder when called to a scene. Why? Should you be involved in a sudden-death situation, it may help you understand why these incredible men and women perform certain tasks and how you could be of help by understanding their focus and goals when assisting the person(s) in need. And, if for no other reason, to appreciate their work, training, and dedication to their profession.

Paramedics and EMS (Emergency Medical Service)

Usually, first responders are summoned to a residence by a family member who dials 9-1-1. First responders can include firefighters, paramedics and EMS, police, chaplains, and a coroner. When first responders arrive on-scene, they immediately ensure the scene is safe for responders. Once secure, a crew member will interview the caller for more information, obtaining the patient's history and gathering his or her medications, if appropriate. The remaining first responders will start treatment, such as putting the patient on oxygen, taking vitals, and putting him or her on a heart monitor. If an IV is needed, it will be started, and medications given.

In contrast, if on arrival, they find the patient with no pulse, they will initiate CPR and follow protocol with defibrillation, a special airway tube, medication, and continued advanced life support while en route to the hospital. If after following protocol there is no response from the patient and he or she has reached end-of-life, law enforcement, the coroner, and a chaplain will be called. This protocol has been practiced hundreds of times through training and "on-scene" calls, so our response has become a well-choreographed rhythm, which allows us to be efficient and effective.

Prior to the use of DNR (Do Not Resuscitate) orders, first responders were required by law to treat any patient they were called to assist. This made for some unpleasant interactions between the family and first responders when someone called 9-1-1 for a terminal patient. Thankfully, responders can now call the hospital and confirm the name and number on the DNR and forgo any treatment, but that was not the case decades ago when I was called out on 9-1-1 calls.

I remember a particular debrief about a young mother who locked the front screen door and refused to let first responders in while she explained her infant child had a terminal disease. It had been ten minutes by the clock since he'd died, and she wouldn't let anyone in until the paramedics promised they would not attempt to revive her baby. What she did was a perfect response to her child's terminal condition, both ethically and legally. It was a very brave thing to do on the worst day of her life. I wished everyone had the ability—in the right circumstance—to do this in my earlier years as a paramedic.

It is a common belief that simply having a DNR statement in your will or trust makes it valid or that creating your own document makes it legal. This is simply not true. A Do-Not-Resuscitate (DNR) order is a legal document that must be completed with and signed off by your physician using an official form for your state of residence. If you do not follow your state's law, your wishes will be challenged at the moment of need. Keep a copy of the DNR on hand at home, and make sure your family members know where it is in the event they need to provide it to first responders.

The Role of a Chaplain

Chaplains respond to counsel, assist, and support victims and witnesses of critical incidents, crises, and other traumatic events. They are specially trained in handling these situations and are available to provide follow-up counseling and intervention for people in a given geographical area. When called upon for larger needs, they may travel to other regions to assist local chaplains, law enforcement, fire departments, and local governments.

In addition to providing support for victims and survivors, chaplains also work with first responders on a professional level, providing critical-incident response, post-traumatic counseling, and other necessary support in crisis-related events. The chaplain team provides immediate, confidential, personal, and family counseling within the framework of non-denominational spiritual guidance to any law enforcement officer, firefighter, EMS responder, department employee, and their families.

The duties of chaplains generally coincide with the following activities and many others:
- Death notifications.
- Suicides, threats, and attempts.
- Fatal and non-fatal accidents.
- Fatal and non-fatal shootings.

- Structure fires.
- Missing persons.
- Drownings.
- SWAT operations.
- Victim/survivor assistance.
- Major disasters.
- Liaison with relief agencies.
- Critical incident debriefings.
- Domestic disturbances.
- Help with family members of departmental personnel.
- Officer deaths, funerals and memorials of on-duty or retired personnel.
- Ceremonies, such as benedictions, graduations, banquets, and weddings.
- Visit sick or injured personnel at home or in the hospital.
- Represent the departments before official bodies upon request.
- Public relations intervention.

One of my many functions as a chaplain was to provide death notifications with law enforcement personnel. This involves notifying the next of kin that a loved one has died. My experience has always been that the person making the notification will make every possible attempt for an in-person notification versus over the phone. This is an exceedingly difficult call or visit for everyone involved, and the officers I worked with were kind and gentle in their delivery of the news. At every possible opportunity, a chaplain will accompany the officer while the officer does the notification. After the officer gives the family member any information they are authorized to give and obtains the information they need in return, they will excuse themselves and depart. At that time, the chaplain remains to assist the family.

My first few callouts as chaplain were for deaths in homes; most were natural deaths, but not all. Then we were asked to do a debriefing for an entire neighborhood that had witnessed a child being struck by a car. It had been a warm summer evening with witnesses congregating and visually taking in the aftermath.

I could tell by the crowd's concern and comments that it would be a long and emotional evening. We used a hall in the neighborhood and split the group into two rooms to keep the numbers more manageable, allowing individuals more time to share and ask questions. Afterward, we offered individual counseling for those interested. It was the first of many debriefings I would participate in.

Early on as a chaplain, I asked Pastor Rick what to say to families. He said, "Pray about it en route. Say, 'Lord, You put me in this position to serve, so what do I say to these grieving family members?'" So, I always prayed on the way to the call that God would put the words in my mouth. If there were no words, I would say nothing. I found that just sitting quietly with someone was all that was needed or wanted at times. This "ministry of presence" can be reassuring to the survivors. And as far as knowing what to do, Chaplain Lee, our lead chaplain, would always say, "Just love on them. Show them love in whatever way they need."

One time, another chaplain and I responded to a death in a residential backyard. An elderly man who was mowing the lawn had collapsed and died. He was lying on his back, with the lawnmower still at his feet. It was obvious that this cowboy, still wearing his cowboy boots, shirt with snaps down the front, jeans, and a rodeo buckle, was lean and used to hard work. His sister was in the house and was inconsolable. He had been living on the family ranch in the mountains when she had asked him to come live with her over concern about him being alone. Now she was blaming herself for his death. There were several upset family members present in the living room with her when I knelt in front of her and spoke.

"You were worried about him and brought him here to live. Look at what he was doing when he died—he was mowing the lawn, working the land. He was not in a rest home or confined to a bed. If he had died at the ranch, how long would it have been before he was found? Days? He died with his boots on. I think that would be what he wanted. I think if he were here, he would say, 'Thank you, sis.'" Then I gave her a big hug.

She held me for a long time and thanked me. As we were leaving, one family member leaned in close to me and whispered, "That was perfect."

The Coroner

I (Rick) met Steven Paris through a mutual friend. I could tell as soon as I spoke with him that I would come to appreciate and value him as a person and coroner investigator for a California sheriff's office. My instincts have proven to be true. In talking with Steven, I found him to be incredibly respectful of others and completely dedicated to his work. He has brought an even greater appreciation from my perspective to his line of work and the men and women who serve our communities.

It is not often that we get a glimpse behind the scenes into the world of a coroner. If your knowledge about the coroner's office is based on what you have seen on TV, then there is much you do not know. Why is it important to understand what the coroner's office and investigators do as a service to their communities? Because you may have experience with a coroner investigator one day. Learning the facts may also assist you in working with a family member or fellow employee one day. Genuinely appreciating people and their professions comes from a greater understanding of their work, and these men and women deserve a greater appreciation.

When a Coroner Gets Involved

I (Steven) am used to being the one person no one wants to meet. Working in a coroner's office means I have the unfortunate duty to inform people of the loss of a loved one. I also have the honor to try to help them through a difficult time.

First, we should get some technical information out of the way. In the United States, there are coroners and medical examiners. Though these agencies can operate differently, they essentially have the same job. Both agencies are there to determine the cause and manner of death. A medical examiner's office is run by a doctor, usually a forensic pathologist. In contrast, a coroner's office is run by an elected official who is not required to have any medical training. In the coroner's office where I work, we utilize a forensic pathologist who makes the medical determination of the cause of death. Coroners in California are required to rely on a doctor to issue the medical cause of death. In summary, both medical examiners and coroners perform the same job. I will be using the term "coroner," but you might have a medical examiner where you live. Most of this information still applies.

One of the first questions I am asked about my profession is, "Why do coroners get involved, and how often are you called out?" Not all deaths need a coroner involved—in fact, most do not. In the county where I work, our office only sees about one-fifth of the deaths in the county. That means if there are 1,500 deaths a year, we only handle about 300 of them. In California, this is spelled out in section 27491 of the government code. Essentially, if your loved one dies of natural causes under the care of a physician, they will not need a coroner. If the death happens at home, a coroner might get involved. If the death can be categorized as anything other than "natural," a coroner is needed.

Cause and Manner of Death

Whether or not the coroner gets involved is based on the cause and manner of death. The cause is the medical reason a person died, such as hypertensive and atherosclerotic cardiovascular disease, fatal cardiac dysrhythmia, or acute intracerebral hematoma. The manner of death is how the person died. There are generally five categories of manners: natural, accidental, suicide, homicide, and undetermined. Some cases are clear-cut; others are not. The following are some examples of non-natural manners of death.

Injury-Related Death

If your loved one is in hospice due to an injury (broken hip is the most common here), this would be an accidental death if the injury is implicated. That means the coroner's office may get involved. Don't be surprised if the hospice nurse has the decedent taken directly to the mortuary, and a few days later, you get a call from the coroner. It happens all the time, and our office will work diligently to get the case cleared up so the family can have services for their loved one.

Sudden Infant Death Syndrome (SIDS)

In the case of Sudden Infant Death Syndrome (SIDS), also known as Sudden Unexpected Infant Death Syndrome (SUIDS) death, additional steps must be taken. The coroner must interview more people, take temperature readings inside the space the child was occupying, and fill out a long checklist. In these cases, coroners are tasked with collecting copious amounts of data for public health so these deaths can be analyzed and hopefully prevented in the future. If you have ever wondered why medical professionals recommended laying your sleeping infant on their back in a crib, only to later recommend laying them on their stomach, it is because standards of care are updated based on the analysis of these cases. Unfortunately, some SIDS/SUIDS cases are left undetermined because we cannot determine the cause of death. That is rare and difficult for everyone involved, but it does happen.

Homicide

If your loved one dies resulting from a homicide (that does not necessarily mean murder), you will face more questions from detectives and coroners. You may also have to wait longer to have your loved one transferred to a mortuary because the decedent is legally considered evidence in a homicide investigation. That does not mean we are going to keep your loved one until the case is finished. It means we must keep them until we have done everything possible to preserve and collect evidence. This may also be the case in any suspicious death. Remember, the coroner is doing a parallel investigation with other law enforcement personnel. The coroner may stop treating the death as suspicious if the law enforcement investigation concludes it is not. The coroner may also issue a manner of death as homicide, even when a law enforcement investigation determines the death is accidental. The reason is not nefarious but simply because, legally, homicide is the death of a person caused by the actions of another person. This might be due to a tragic accident. In contrast, murder is the unlawful killing of a person by another person. The key distinction is *unlawful*.

In the event of a homicide, the next of kin may be notified by the investigating agency, or the coroner and the investigating agency will make the notification together. The investigating agency may want to do the notification to gather information about the decedent that is pertinent to their investigation. These investigations are complex and require several agencies to work together. This also means any of the agencies may do a press release, or they may coordinate the press response so the information only comes from one source.

Suicide

On August 4, 2015, I (Rick) officiated a memorial service for a young man named Kris. It was well attended by family and friends, many of whom were surprised to hear that he had taken his own life. His father, Jeff, was devastated. He'd had conversations with Kris that indicated the depth of his issues, but Kris always said, "Nothing is wrong" or "There's nothing to worry about." Jeff had watched and reached out, not imagining any problem(s) couldn't be worked out. In hindsight, Jeff told me, "If there is even a hint that hopelessness might be present, that's when a deep, intimate conversation should take place." When Kris made that final decision to end his life, everyone, including Jeff, was shocked. Jeff continued his story saying, "The anguish and pain were so hard. I couldn't even imagine why this happened. How could this happen? I felt shock, anger, and guilt, which left me paralyzed. The deepest and most lasting of these emotions was the feeling of guilt—the feeling of not doing enough to help or asking enough questions or the big question, are you without hope?"

Unfortunately, suicide occurs daily throughout our country. Rather than dwell on how or why this happens, I asked Jeff about how he processed through the death of his son and how he recovered—and to what degree he has recovered. Processing through death can, and often does, begin at the scene. Jeff met the chaplain who was dispatched along with the police. As the police systematically went through their process of recovering information, Jeff talked and prayed with the chaplain. As a Christian, Jeff put his hand on Kris's body as he was taken to the vehicle for transportation, saying, "Please, Lord, welcome Kris into his heavenly home."

> This was the beginning of Jeff's recovery—his faith. Faith gave him hope that death, no matter the manner, is not the end.

What a Coroner Does

When I (Steven) arrive on-scene, if there is family present, I introduce myself and explain my role. Then I invite questions from the family. I usually get a brief statement about what happened and any pertinent medical history about the decedent. After this initial encounter, I go to the deceased. I conduct an examination to look for injuries and see if the information I gathered matches what I am seeing on the deceased. I take photographs and document injuries, bruises, and the condition of the deceased. I am not a doctor, and I am not conducting an autopsy; I am simply documenting the condition of the deceased at that precise moment. I am gathering information to give to the doctor so the doctor can make a medical determination. At the scene (at least in California), you will notice the police do not touch the deceased. That is because they are not allowed to. Police officers are not deputy coroners. Accordingly, the only time a police officer in California can touch the deceased is at the scene of a traffic collision, and that is only to check for a donor card. Other than that, the officers must wait for the coroner.

After I conduct my examination, I talk to the family or witnesses again. I confirm information and ensure I have accurately captured the chain of events. The transport service comes to the scene and takes the deceased to the morgue (if the coroner decides to take the decedent).

Once back at the coroner's office, I start writing my report and requesting other documents I might need, such as medical records. Once the information is collected, I forward the communication to the pathologist. The pathologist may review the records and determine the cause of death, schedule an examination of the decedent, or ask the investigator for a more specific follow-up investigation. If the pathologist determines there needs to be an autopsy to determine cause, or if the case requires an autopsy (murder), an autopsy is scheduled by the coroner.

If there is no family at the scene, my priority after processing the scene is to locate and notify the next of kin. This is important because the family needs to know so they can both grieve and decide on the appropriate disposition of the remains.

All coroner cases have these same priorities, regardless of the circumstances. Sometimes progress takes longer due to the circumstances (such as when a decedent is discovered in the woods after an extended period). Our job requires us to apply the same steps and care to every case, no matter the age of the decedent or how the decedent died. Some cases get extra steps added in, but those are less frequent.

Coroner Costs

One question the coroner's office is asked frequently is about costs. Some jurisdictions charge storage fees for housing the decedent; ours is not one of those jurisdictions. Remember, the coroner's office is a government service, so the work they do is covered by your tax dollars. We do not charge families for autopsies, lab work, or our investigation. That also means we do not perform autopsies on request. We do not want to spend taxpayer money to do unnecessary procedures, so we take the least invasive means possible to determine the cause of death. If you and your family honestly believe an autopsy is needed and the coroner is not going to perform one, you have the option of paying for a private autopsy. This can be expensive and is usually done at the mortuary, not the coroner's office. Be warned, if a private autopsy is done and the performing doctor disagrees with the coroner about the cause of death, his or her opinion does not change the death certificate, which is completed based on the coroner's determination. In fact, the coroner can take jurisdiction of a death and change the cause of death, even if the cause has already been entered by a private physician.

One cost the family must usually bear is the cost of certified death certificates. The coroner does not generate these documents and therefore does not charge you for them. They are available from your county recorder's office, but most mortuaries provide a certain number of copies with the burial/cremation services they provide.

Action Steps

- If you have experienced the sudden death of a loved one or friend, reach out to your house of worship, a city or hospital chaplain, or someone who can guide you through the next steps.
- Read the Survivor Checklist in the appendix of this book. This is a helpful tool to keep you on track with items that need your attention, both now and later.
- Have a discussion with your physician to see if a DNR is right for you. If so, complete the necessary paperwork (following your state's laws) and inform your family of your decision and the location of the document.

CHAPTER 6

Coping with Miscarriage, Stillbirth, and Infant Loss

At twenty-one and twenty-two weeks pregnant, Cassie and Carolyn received devastating news about their firstborn children; two different women, two different circumstances, same outcome.

Carolyn was celebrating her wedding anniversary at Lake Tahoe when she began experiencing contractions. The next day back in her hometown, from the doctor's office, a nurse pushed her across the parking lot in a wheelchair to the hospital. Through the tears and fear, Carolyn asked *Will my baby be, okay?* In the ED, doctors and nurses surrounded her. The noise and rapid questions were overwhelming, but she answered the best she could. Despite heroic efforts by the hospital staff, Carolyn's son, Steven, entered this world prematurely. Fewer than two minutes after taking his first breath, he breathed his last.

Since this was Carolyn's first experience with pregnancy and delivery, the emotions of the experience were overwhelming, and she had no idea what to expect next. The nurses spoke to her calmly—even though they must have been feeling the emotional pain themselves—saying, "We are going to move you to the labor/ delivery room where you can spend as much time with your baby as you like." They cleaned Steven and put him on Carolyn's chest, wrapped in a blanket with a sock hat covering his little head. He weighed just twelve ounces.

Cassie never expected her routine check-up to lead to a trip to the hospital. Instead of hearing her daughter's heartbeat, the diagnosis of leaking amniotic fluid confirmed the worst. The options her doctor gave her were grim. "You can go home on bed rest and take steroids for lung enhancement, or you can go to a different doctor and terminate the pregnancy." Ultimately, the choice would be taken out of her hands, as her labor progressed. Like a plan that had been put in place without her consent, her daughter, Kairi, entered the world at one pound, nine inches long, but without the familiar cry. As Cassie told me, "I immediately closed up. I did not want this to be happening. The nurse was so compassionate, but I had already closed the world off."

Carolyn and Cassie both experienced the shock and disbelief that often accompanies the unexpected loss of a preborn child. Cassie said, "I felt with modern medicine and technology, they could do anything to prevent losing my baby. Even if something were wrong, they could fix it." But before twenty-four weeks gestation, both babies had little chance of survival. Yet as nurses placed their babies on their chests after birth, both Carolyn and Cassie experienced movement and connection—however brief.

Carolyn and Cassie are not alone. "The National Institutes of Health estimates that 15 to 20 percent of known pregnancies in the United States result in miscarriage."[1] Like so many women, they faced a monumental emotional journey—one with emotions so strong that they can eclipse reality and paralyze your thinking, causing an emotional shutdown to cope with unbearable loss. There could not be a more intense time to be forced to make decisions, yet many standard end-of-life decisions also apply to the death of the preborn and infant. What funeral home will you use? Cremation or casket? A service by an officiant or simple interment without a service? Some of these decisions take time, but most parents feel pressured to make decisions then, all while doing their best to process all that has happened in such a short time frame.

Alongside those decisions begins the grief journey—one unique to pregnancy loss because it so often goes unrecognized or unseen. Grief over the death of a living child or adult whom others knew and loved is acknowledged, validated, and remembered. The life of a preborn child is physically experienced only by the mother, who may not even share the news of a miscarriage with her friends and family. Her and her partner's grief journey can be invisible or even considered less valid because the life of their child was so short. Yet this loss is life-altering. Grief over a life hoped for yet never lived can be just as deep as any other loss of a loved one.

My friend Dr. John Armstrong, a compassionate and experienced obstetrician, has seen the devastation on the faces of parents who have lost a preborn child and sensed the profound loss in these circumstances as their caregiver. In his twenty-six years as an obstetrician, Dr. John has been present at over 6,000 births. When Dr. John and I talked about this chapter, I asked him to share less about the medical side of his profession because of the complexity of the topic but rather more about emotional healing and myths surrounding miscarriages and stillbirths. Here is Dr. John sharing his professional experience.

Questions without Answers

Several questions arise after the initial news is revealed about a miscarriage or stillbirth. Why? How? When? Did I (the mother) or the medical team do something wrong, or could there have been a proactive measure taken to prevent this tragedy? There may have been trauma or medical risk factors that played a part, but without obvious reasons, we usually cannot answer the question of why with certainty. These questions should certainly be explored with your physician for your personal health and future family planning.

Almost all the patients and their partners I have worked with who have encountered pregnancy loss have expressed some level of uncertainty, guilt, regret, remorse, blame, and fault-finding. In the process of exploring the many questions and emotions that arise, there is a tendency to stay focused on the what-ifs. As a mother reflects, she may say, "Maybe I should not have had a sip of wine." "Perhaps if I'd created a calmer atmosphere at home or work, this wouldn't have happened." "What if I had had better nutrition?" As she processes, her questions may go deeper. "Is God punishing me?" "Have I disappointed my partner or family?" At some point, questions arise about a future pregnancy. "When can I try again; what are my chances of a similar occurrence, and how can I handle the uncertainty?" Fortunately, most miscarriages and stillbirths are not repetitive, and the future is reasonably bright to have a healthy child. Others may choose not to try again and refocus on their existing family structure or consider adoption. There is time to evaluate and decide what is best.

Even parents who successfully process their grief and guilt may still have a sense of loss. Grief is a personal journey, and the duration and intensity will vary by individual. Your grief journey and decisions may be influenced by your personal convictions.

Human Life: Legal Definitions and Personal Convictions

For this chapter, I (Rick) will purposely avoid the conversation about abortion because this topic is different than miscarriage and stillbirth. I will focus more on guiding you through the end-of-life decisions pertaining to miscarriage and stillbirths by asking questions and offering insight as a father and pastor. I do, however, feel there are questions that need to be addressed for a person of faith when a miscarriage or stillbirth occurs. If you are not a person of faith, then you can either ignore these comments or explore the foundation of your personal convictions to assist you when making decisions after a miscarriage or stillbirth occurs. Deciding what you believe in advance will guide you through some of this decision-making. Because laws, personal convictions, and emotions play such a significant role in the decision-making process for miscarriages and stillbirths, having a team of people helping with research on this topic—including your friends and family, medical professional, and spiritual leader—will assist you in your ultimate decisions.

When faced with these decisions, first, your state law will dictate your options, and then your personal convictions about human life will determine your decisions. As an ordained Christian pastor, I have my own firm beliefs, but I have purposely avoided promoting a particular religious faith or house of worship because that is not what this book is about. My purpose for authoring this book is to offer facts that empower the reader to take steps forward with confidence. With that in mind, I offer the following information about miscarriage and stillbirth through the lens of our legal system and medical community.

Gestation period for the infant is the prominent defining factor in differentiating between miscarriage and stillbirth. The loss of a baby twenty weeks or younger is normally considered a miscarriage, whether death occurs before birth, at birth, or shortly after birth. Some states include weight as a contributing factor and define the gestation period by twenty-four or twenty-six weeks. Some states require the attending physician to report miscarriages within ten days, while other states do not require reporting. In the case of miscarriages, a death certificate is not usually required. Check with your state law for accuracy since policies relating to all these factors can vary and change with some frequency.

A loss after twenty weeks is considered a stillbirth. To be considered stillbirth, the baby's life must have terminated before birth. In this case, a death certificate is often required. Again, these definitions and requirements can vary from state to state, so check your state's laws.

Steps to Take after a Pregnancy Loss

Give Your Baby a Name

Many parents, like Carolyn and Cassie, find it helpful to name their baby. A name brings a sense of personhood and can make it easier to refer to the baby in conversation. If your situation requires a death certificate, you'll need to identify your baby with a name. State laws will dictate your choices, but most states offer multiple options. For my state, California, the baby can be recorded as Baby Smith (no first name) or by a given first and last name (Jane Smith) for the document. If the parents have two different last names, then both last names can be listed, such as Baby Jones Smith.

Take Time and Take Pictures

After Kairi was cleaned and placed once again on Cassie's chest, the nurses offered to take pictures—which is normal and can serve as a first step in emotional healing—along with offering the family as much time together as desired. In the overwhelming trauma of the situation, Cassie declined the pictures, which she later said was one of her great regrets, in addition to not spending more time with Kairi.

Carolyn had pictures taken of Steven, but as she reflected on the experience much later, she wished she would have taken more time and photos with Steven. In the moment, it may feel awkward or unnecessary, but it's a time you'll never get back. Many hospitals also offer keepsakes, such as a handprint or footprint, ID bracelet, stocking hat, or receiving blanket. Before you refuse a keepsake, think about if it will be important to you later in remembering your child.

Decide on Disposition

What happens to your baby's body after a miscarriage or stillbirth? Some individual states address what to do with "fetal remains," which is a legal and medical community terminology—not mine. House Bill 1890 Pennsylvania 2019, titled "Final Disposition of Fetal Remains,"[1] talks specifically about this and promotes mandatory burial or cremation for the human remains. A 2018 report by the Office of Legislative Research in Connecticut on miscarriage burial laws had this to say:

> *When a miscarriage occurs, health care facilities generally dispose of the remains as medical waste. However, some parents have expressed the desire to control the disposition of fetal remains and choose to bury or cremate them. It appears that*

*most states, including Connecticut, do not have
laws addressing the issue, although health care
facilities or state agencies may adopt related policies. States that do have such laws either require
health care facilities to notify parents of their
ability to bury or cremate their miscarried fetus
or reference parents' ability to do so.*[2]

It is too extensive a work to list each state's position here, as
laws are proposed and changed regularly, so researching on your
own will educate and empower you to be aware of local laws.

These state guidelines use language that reflects a perspective
that considers the baby "medical waste." If your personal convictions align with this belief that the baby is just fetal remains
or medical waste, you may believe that disposition is the hospital's responsibility. On the other hand, if you hold the belief that
human life is just that—human life—then the remains would not
be considered medical waste but rather a baby that deserves to be
buried with dignity and honor. My point here is this: Your decision-making about having a burial, cremation, or service to honor
your baby will be guided largely by your personal convictions
and cultural norms, emotional state, finances, family, and additional factors.

Both Cassie and Carolyn chose to bury their babies. Kairi's
interment included a graveside service officiated by a pastor,
and the tiny casket was lowered in the ground within the infant
section at a local cemetery where she was honored with dignity.
Once Carolyn and her husband obtained the death certificate for
Steven, which happened quickly since an autopsy or other medical
examination was not needed, he was laid to rest in a niche in the
columbarium at a cemetery within a few miles of their home. The
cemetery they chose had a section for infants where parents were
not charged for interment, a gift that became part of their healing.

If you choose to have your baby buried or cremated, you
will need to contact a funeral home, as with any other death. As
Carolyn experienced, many funeral homes offer services free-of-
cost for infant loss. Cemeteries often have a special infant section

with plots available free-of-charge. You will likely have the option of burial with a casket in the ground or in a niche within a columbarium. Organizations like the Emma & Evan Foundation (https://www.evefoundation.org/) transform donated wedding dresses into beautiful infant burial gowns, also called angel gowns. These gowns are offered to hospitals, birthing centers, funeral homes, and directly to grieving families completely free of charge. If you choose to have your baby cremated, a disposition permit may be required if you want to spread ashes. Research your own state laws or ask your funeral home about disposition regulations.

What happens to the baby resulting from a miscarriage if the parent(s) choose not to have cremation at a mortuary or burial at a cemetery? The answer is a licensed third party receives the baby from the medical facility and cremates them.

Plan an Acknowledgment of Life Service

Whether or not to formally acknowledge the loss of your baby is a personal choice, but as a pastor who has sat with dozens of grieving families, I have seen the value of a service in bringing closure and healing. The purpose of a service is to acknowledge the person and eulogize that person, while identifying the loss with a date, time, and place as a reference point. Not having a formal gathering of some type can, and quite often does, leave the family lingering without a reference point when people come together for a specific purpose. To be clear, I am not saying that every miscarriage mandates a funeral, graveside service, or memorial, but I am saying that whether it is the parents, family, or a larger gathering, acknowledging the loss helps with the grief journey while honoring the baby with dignity. The service you design could be as simple as meeting with family and friends in your backyard and sharing your grief or story. Or, it could be just you as the parents setting aside time to talk, identify the loss, and express your view through your chosen faith, tradition, or counseling. This simple acknowledgment of life can be a major part of your grief journey to recovery.

Carolyn and Cassie both held services for their children. Carolyn realized later that:

> *. . . the service was more for us than anyone else. Steven's service was one tiny step in the closure process for us. As I reflect upon his funeral service now, years later, I realize how big of a step it was in the healing process for both my husband and me. Without a service, I can only imagine the difficulty in being able to identify a date, time, place, and gathering that signified his existence, our relation- ship, and the depth of love we had for Steven.*

Reach Out for Support

Emotional recovery is a journey and one that you shouldn't walk alone. In the case of pregnancy loss, all the normal emotions of grief—shock, anger, depression, and denial—are complicated by the profound physical transition of birth and all the associated hormonal shifts. In the case of miscarriage and stillbirth, you are still at risk for postpartum depression. Resource materials and pro- grams are available for all impacted by a pregnancy loss to gain accurate information, a listening ear, and support. Carolyn shared the following about her grief journey:

> *Within a few weeks, I was back at work, despite my employer offering more time off for bereavement. It was my decision to step back into a routine, but the numbness was relentless, lingering, and nagging at my heart for an additional three to four months. Family members, friends, and co-workers made comments that were well-intentioned but hurtful. With each comment, I found my emotions being triggered. I was raw, recovering, and felt lost daily, but I also knew I had to keep taking a step forward in my emotional recovery. Some days were good;*

some days were bad. I couldn't predict it, and my emotional healing wasn't linear. Around month eight or nine, I found myself beginning to smile and laugh again while I engaged in conversations that provided moments of hope and happiness.

Chaplains

Many hospitals have chaplains who are available to meet with you during this difficult time. A hospital social worker can provide a list of community resources available to you for support after you leave the hospital.

Counseling

Specialized individual counseling is available for those who need help with anxiety, depression, or worsening of prior mental health issues. You have been through a traumatic loss; there is no shame in reaching out and asking for help—when you're ready.

After Cassie was discharged from the hospital, she had access to one year of counseling through her county. As part of her journey, Cassie had three or four grief counseling sessions, but "didn't get anything out of it." It is normal to reject counseling initially but later learn its value and become emotionally prepared to receive this care.

> *You have to be ready to receive help*, and if it is too early in the journey, you may not get the full benefit out of counseling. However, don't delay too long. If you need a therapist, connect with one earlier rather than later.

Don't forget your partner in the grief journey. Couples often grieve differently, and the loss of your baby can put a strain on your relationship. Too often, couples drift apart from one another rather than rally together. You need your space, but you also need to be together, sharing your feelings, supporting one another, and talking together regularly. Take this journey together and pursue couples' counseling if needed.

Community

I (Rick) recall the day Cassie and her husband, Brian, first started to attend our church. They were looking for answers to help navigate the emotional journey and replace the feeling of emptiness. Both Cassie and Brian connected with people who facilitated their journey to discovering what they were looking for—answers and hope!

Both Cassie and Carolyn found solace in their faith. Carolyn told me, "Our faith was a tremendous anchor for us as we searched for the answer to the question *why*. I learned that having a community of family and friends around you is extremely important. I could not imagine going through this without their support and without my relationship with God." If you are a person of faith, the love and care of your spiritual community can bring comfort during this difficult time, show you the grace you need, and help you find peace.

As Carolyn and I talked about her experience, I asked, "What did you learn from this?" Carolyn shared this with me:

> *We will never know the reason why Steven's life was so abrupt. I would drive myself crazy if I spent the rest of my life trying to figure out why this happened. Don't live in a world where you say, "I should have . . ." This can be destructive for you. I learned that there is a healthy way to grieve and an unhealthy way. Do not sweep this under the proverbial carpet. It doesn't work! Grieving is a process, and I learned the process. Give yourself a lot of grace because you will need it.*

If you ask Carolyn today how many children she has, she will say three: Steven and her two daughters. Steven is part of her family.

> ### Action Steps
>
> - Examine your personal convictions about pregnancy and human life to help you with the decisions you may face, now or in the future.
> - If you have experienced the loss of your preborn child, identify and take the next step on your grief journey, perhaps by seeking counseling or connecting to a faith community.
> - Reach out to someone you know who has experienced a pregnancy loss. If you've had your own loss, they may offer understanding and insight. If you haven't experienced a loss, you can learn from their journey.

CHAPTER 7

Clarifying Bereavement Leave

I f there was ever a time that I needed time off from work, it was then. When my brother, wife, and mom died all within an eighteen-month period, the shock and grief with each family member's passing were immense. The time I needed for grieving, along with the immediate responsibilities pertaining to end-of-life administrative and legal responsibilities, left no time or energy for work. Gratefully, I turned to my employee benefits for bereavement leave.

I was familiar with company bereavement policies (CBPs), having written numerous policies in both business and ministry as a campus pastor. So, why is it important to know the details of your CBP? Simple: Knowing in advance, while you can process clearly, allows you time to formulate a plan and a negotiation strategy. While under stress, your cognitive skills are reduced; therefore, your best planning may be inadequate. Have you ever attempted to formulate a plan or comprehend a complex document while under stress? If so, then you know your limitations are real and can hamper your desired outcome. This chapter will help you prepare to approach your employer. Let's explore this topic together.

Pre-Need

What Is Bereavement Leave?

To understand *bereavement leave*, we first need to define bereavement. My experience as a pastor, and one who has lost four close family members, is that I have become acquainted with grief, mourning, and bereavement. In its simplest form—although the emotions and outward expression of each are intense—grief can be understood as the way one processes through the multitude of emotions that occur after a loss. It's an emotional journey that includes our actions and how we express ourselves. The grief journey shares similarities within a culture, although there is a uniqueness with individuals on how they process through their grief. For more information on grief, see chapter thirteen.

Mourning, an intricately linked part of the grief process, is how we show our grief in public, which I learned firsthand. Mourning can be influenced by our belief system and personal convictions through cultural norms or faith customs. This is not to say that all our outward expressions of grief are motivated by someone else or institutionalized through affiliations, but they can influence our mourning. Examples of these cultural norms or faith customs could be a funeral/memorial followed with a reception or annual gatherings to remember the loss of a loved one. In addition, emblems we strategically place at home or workplace to remember our loss can be examples of mourning.

Bereavement, as I experienced in my grief and mourning, is what one may call the entire journey itself. Bereavement has the potential to last for months or years because it is all-encompassing. But here is where the delineation of grief and mourning versus bereavement leave or policy conflict. If bereavement within our workplace has been assigned a timeline, then who decides what is a healthy timeline, and how does our employer define that timeline? With administrative needs that can last for years, bereavement can slow or hold a person in his or her grief journey much longer than anticipated. I found this to be initially true after my wife's death, as I still have administrative duties more than four-teen years later due to family trusts.

To better understand what bereavement is and then how to view your organization's policy regarding it, I have developed through personal experience and research my own definition of bereavement:

> Bereavement can vary from person to person, but the root understanding for most involves loss. Bereavement is rightfully associated with the intense emotions one feels after the loss of a loved one, and it often involves the administrative work associated with end-of-life. Bereavement encompasses *the whole journey* of loss, with incremental steps forward highlighted by identifiable components—grief, mourning, and administrative tasks.

Understanding Policy vs. Law

Recently, I had a conversation with my sister-in-law, Kim, who worked in the HR department for her organization and specifically handled bereavement requests and similar HR policies. She made a comment to me that has become the essence of this chapter: "Employers focus on benefits for the sick and the family, but when it comes to death, the benefits stop." She's right. The Department of Labor, a federal agency, offers a host of benefits under the Family Medical Leave Act (FMLA), but the law is silent when it comes to bereavement leave. According to the Employment Law Handbook website:[1]

Currently, there are no federal laws that require employers to provide employees either paid or unpaid leave. Also, only one state, Oregon, has passed a law requiring employers to provide bereavement leave (it took effect January 1, 2014). The other forty-nine states, plus the District of Columbia, do not require employers to provide employees either paid or unpaid bereavement leave. Employers, at their discretion, may maintain bereavement leave policies or practices and, in certain circumstances, may be obligated to comply with their established policy or practice. Employers must comply with bereavement leave policies that are part of individual employment contracts or collective bargaining agreements.

Although employers are not required by law to offer bereavement leave, many do in their company policies. As part of my research, I sent out a survey to over fifty people who work both in private industry and as government employees with specific questions about their organizations' CBP. Here is what I learned from these questions:

- Seventy percent of those surveyed say their company offers bereavement leave.
- Over one-third surveyed said their standard bereavement leave allows for one to three days paid time off (PTO).
- One-third surveyed said their standard bereavement leave allows for four to six days PTO.
- Less than half surveyed said they can donate time to another employee from their personal PTO, extending their fellow employees' bereavement leave.
- More than half surveyed said they can combine their own PTO along with bereavement leave, allowing for more time away.
- Only a few surveyed said they do not have a CBP, so bereavement leave is left for negotiation.

I recall working with one family where the primary income earner had died. The surviving family was financially sound thanks to diligent work prior to death, but the surviving spouse struggled daily to make the simplest decisions, let alone become a leader in the family business. How much time is needed for someone to emotionally recover in this scenario? It depends upon the person, but one to three days is grossly insufficient when you consider funeral preparation, grieving, legal work, discovering a new normal, and taking the lead in the family business. The same is true, to a degree, for the person returning to work as an employee.

At-Need

Negotiating Bereavement Leave

Negotiation is possible even if there is no written policy or in addition to a written policy, unless the company specifically states that negotiation is not permissible within their guidelines. The following suggestions for maximizing bereavement leave assume that negotiation is a possibility.

Combine with PTO

By requesting to combine paid bereavement leave with your PTO, the likelihood of having an extended time off to grieve, plan a service, and complete the necessary administrative work is substantially increased. With this simple act of negotiation, you have potentially just increased your time off from one to three days to two to four weeks.

Request Donated Time

If you are short of PTO and your paid bereavement leave is the standard one to three days, then consider asking your HR director to allow fellow employees to donate a portion of their PTO to be used in conjunction with your paid bereavement leave. It is important to broach this subject with your employer in a thoughtful, well-organized manner. To the best of your ability, answer the following questions before approaching your supervisor or HR Director.

- How will your absence affect your employer?
- Are there people who can assume your duties in your absence?
- Are other colleagues currently using PTO or sick time, and so on?
- How will your department manage with one more person off work?

Taking all this into consideration has the potential to firmly establish your position in negotiation.

From my own experience, this is a time when employers can build a positive image by being willing to work with an employee. In addition, it can boost company morale when an employer offers flexibility to accommodate an employee in their time of need. But keep in mind, those who abuse company benefits can potentially put this benefit at risk for everyone else. So, your intent, temperament, and style when approaching your employer can set the future standard of flexibility and possibly open the door for exactly what you need—more time off.

Ask in Advance

If you are not successful in acquiring the time off needed beyond the standard one to three days of bereavement leave, consider asking for PTO at the earliest opportunity to attend a memorial service planned for a future date. Submitting this request early will help in your negotiation later. For clarification, the difference between a funeral and a memorial is as such: Regarding funerals, the deceased is buried in the ground or mausoleum and takes place within three to ten days following death. Regarding memorials, the deceased is already buried (or cremated), and the service may take place a week to a month or longer after death.

Ask for Assistance

When sudden death occurs, leaving you to plan at-need, it is highly likely that you are not thinking clearly, so your request for time off may seem abrupt or panicked, which is normal. To assist you under this stress, consider having a family member or trusted friend who is able to think clearly assist you.

Discuss Re-Entry to Work

Losing a loved one is difficult, and quite often, the standard time off allowed is not sufficient, so consider asking to work part-time for a negotiated period as part of your re-entry plan. Do keep in mind that if your job is a full-time position, an extended time off could present a challenge for the company, so be gracious and accept what is offered through negotiation. Any additional time off is better than nothing.

The Returning Employee

The grief journey is unique, so few colleagues will know exactly how you are feeling, although some may personally know the journey well. Therefore, communicating to your colleagues how you are feeling through an email or note in advance of returning to work may prepare them and ease the awkwardness of the reunion. Remember, our culture does little to train people how to respond to death; therefore, helping them understand your journey will be appreciated. Keep your note short, and only write what you want your colleagues to know about your journey. A note that invites them to join your journey builds bridges and partnerships.

It is a good idea to send this note to your supervisor or company owner before sending it to your colleagues. Honoring them first can set the tone both before and upon your return to work. There is a saying for times like this: "Good paper makes good friends!" Applying this to your return-to-work means honoring those in key positions and can create alliances. In return, they may become an advocate for you.

Here is a template for you to consider. Feel empowered to change the wording of the letter to fit your style, circumstance, and situation.

My friends and colleagues,
As you are aware, I recently suffered a loss in my life through the death of my (relationship), (name). My grief journey could take weeks or months or more. I'm doing the best I can. Upon my return to work, it may be awkward for both you and me, so a simple "welcome back" would be appreciated since lengthy conversations and explanations may be too emotional for me right

now. I will discover my new normal over time, but for now, I want you to know that I may have tears while at my desk, or in the print room, or on break, and for no apparent reason other than grieving. This is not a reflection on you but rather part of my journey, and although difficult, it's normal and healthy.

I am okay with you asking me to go to lunch or meet after work; in fact, I invite it, but at the same time, please don't be offended if I say no. Part of the grief journey is literally taking each day and hour as they come, which means today could be a good day, and tomorrow not so good.

There may be times when I make mistakes with my work, so I ask you to kindly point those out to me. I would rather we work together as a team rather than have my mistakes cause additional work for you and me. This, too, is part of the grief journey—me trying to focus, and you helping when appropriate and when needed.

I appreciate your understanding, and hopefully, this note provides some insight into where I am emotionally and in the grief journey. Please join me as we understand more about this journey together.

Sincerely,

(Your name)

The Returning Colleague

What do I say to a colleague who just experienced a loss in his or her life? Too often in our culture, a lack of training and our desire to help the person feel better by saying the "right thing," can compound the person's grief and create an awkwardness that is undeniable. Unfortunately, this can cause a strained relationship at minimum, or worse, leave a lasting emotional scar.

When my wife, Susie, died, I was able to take the three days of bereavement leave offered and combine it with PTO for a total of three paid weeks off. I needed it, and probably even more time in hindsight. One of the toughest days in my life was my first Sunday back to church. The love being poured out by friends and the church family as I greeted them in the lobby was overwhelming.

As each service began, I found myself weeping uncontrollably in my office since I was not preaching and could find solace in being alone. This was grieving for me; the emotions that surfaced were intense with loss, and at the same time, I felt so loved. However, there were some comments made that hurt, not because the people had ill intent, but rather because they did not know what to say.

Through my end-of-life experiences with my brother, wife, and mom, I learned the value of not trying to fix someone or have the perfect comment, but rather how sometimes the less said, the better. Based on both my personal experiences and professional research, I offer you these thoughts that may help guide you in your responses. These are honoring, open-ended statements that allow the survivor to talk when you greet them, later, or not at all—hopefully without awkwardness. I would like to point out, however, that saying nothing to avoid the subject matter and their grief could communicate that you do not care. Showing sympathy and interest communicates that you care (provided you share appropriately).

Appropriate Responses to Returning Colleagues That Show You Care

Using one of these statements to your colleague will acknowledge his or her loss while showing sympathy on your part. Remember, it is not your job to fix him or her, nor can you.

- If you know the person well, consider saying, *"I love you, (insert colleague's name). I am so happy to see you again. We have missed you."* With this statement, you are not avoiding his or her loss, but rather are focusing on your colleague or employee, which he or she may really appreciate.

- *"(Insert colleague's name), I cannot imagine your grief, but I am here to help if you need anything from me."* With this statement, your integrity is on the line; only offer

103

to help if you really mean it. An insincere offer is no help at all.

- *"It is so good to have you back. I would love to hear more about (insert deceased's name) if you would like to share, and when the time is right."* Offering your employees or colleagues a chance to share about their loved one at a future date of their choosing puts them in control of the situation and gives them a chance to prepare emotionally.

- *"How are you doing today, (insert colleague's name)?"* Every day is a journey when grieving, so identifying "today" as the moment in time referenced allows the person to share his or her thoughts at that specific moment rather than retrace the past or project what might be in the future. Retracing the past can be painful and exhausting.

- If the person is a person of faith—and you are as well— consider saying, *"(insert colleague's name), I have been praying for you and your family and will continue to do so. If you have specific prayer needs and would like to share them, I would love to honor you with additional prayer when you are ready."* If the person has something to share, thank him or her, and then pray later when you are alone. If he or she never gets back to you with a specific prayer, pray for general emotional health and other needs known to you without asking for additional personal information.

If You Are the Employee's Supervisor or Employer, Consider These Responses:

- *"(Insert colleague's name), welcome back. We have missed you. I want to be sensitive to your emotions and the overwhelming feeling of being back. How can I work with you as a slow introduction back?"* As a supervisor or employer, this single statement or approach will communicate to your colleague that you care. Without a planned or slow approach, you may communicate to the employee that his or her work is the only thing that matters. Choose wisely how you treat a returning colleague after bereavement leave.

- *"(Insert colleague's name), welcome back. We have missed you. I want to be sensitive to your emotions as you return to work. How can I work with you over the coming days or weeks, or would you prefer I do nothing? You can change your mind at any time."* This approach allows your colleague to choose an approach that might work well for him or her today but with the flexibility to change as needed.

- *"(Insert colleague's name), please accept my condolences over your (insert relationship to employee or their name) passing. I acknowledge this and want to work with you. Can I slowly bring you up to speed with work? Then we can talk about getting you started but with the understanding that I would like your input on how much and how fast this happens. Is that okay?"* Through my own personal experience, bringing the employee up to speed slowly for a week or two will allow him or her to engage in what he or she can accomplish to build confidence without being overwhelmed. This can both create good company morale and show you care about the person. Without this approach, you can anticipate mistakes, a slower recovery at work with reduced productivity, and potential company morale issues.

Another helpful suggestion is not to be afraid to say the deceased's name when speaking to your friend or colleague. Often, well-meaning people will shy away from speaking the name of the deceased. Perhaps they think it will be too hard for the grieving person to hear. But usually, the opposite is true. Survivors have told me how grateful they are to hear their loved one's name spoken. They are glad that the name and memory of their loved one are being preserved.

What NOT to Say to Returning Colleagues after Their Bereavement Leave

- *"I know exactly how you feel. My (insert title) died and I felt . . ."* This statement is all about you. Avoid it like the plague!

- *"At least (insert deceased's name or title) isn't in pain any longer."* True, but your co-worker is! Avoid this statement completely.

- *"Be strong; you will survive this."* Keeping that façade of strength can be harmful since it is just that—a façade. Grieving people need to grieve. Encouraging people to create a façade is only encouraging them to postpone their grief.

- *"Give it time, and you will feel better. This won't last forever."* Time alone does not heal all wounds. There are many things a grieving person can do along the path to recovery, but it is a choice, and few invest in this journey successfully because their goal is to get through it quickly, not effectively.

- *"We're so happy you are back. Work has been hard with you gone."* This communicates that the employee is only worth as much as his or her work, and this statement can easily be taken by the survivor to mean it is his or her fault the workplace has been disrupted. This is an undeserved burden that a grieving person should never have to shoulder.

A note for the employer and colleagues of a returning employee: Remember that your co-worker is on a journey working through his or her grief. Those within the proximity of the person grieving are also on this journey by default. Like the grieving person, you, too, must make a choice on how you respond. Your grace-filled responses and compassion can be part of his or her journey that is cherished and remembered as welcoming and part of the healing process.

Action Steps

- Read and familiarize yourself with your company's bereavement policy. If the end-of-life of a loved one is imminent, understanding your CBP and preparing your request in advance will empower you to present your need in an organized fashion with clarity and accuracy.
- If sudden death has occurred, schedule a meeting with your HR Director or supervisor to negotiate bereavement leave. In addition, ask if you can revisit this conversation within a given period of time, such as one week, to revise your decision and extend or alter your agreed-upon plans.
- If you are currently on bereavement leave, develop a plan for re-entry into the workplace.

CHAPTER 8

Choosing the Right Funeral Home

"What makes one funeral home better than another?" the survivors ask. "Don't they all do the same thing?" As a pastor, I'm often asked to recommend funeral homes, but I hesitate to do so, and for good reason.

In this chapter, we'll take a closer look at this industry of funeral homes and mortuaries to answer those questions. The vast majority of us will visit a funeral home at some point in our lives. If you are planning pre-need, you have the advantage of learning about what's involved while you are thinking clearly rather than while you are confused, grief-stricken, and paralyzed with emotions. The benefit of time allows you to make informed decisions based on research and family discussions. If you are planning at-need when a death has just occurred (quite often unexpected, with no advance planning in place), funeral or memorial planning must take place in the midst of confusion and the pain of grieving. If that's your situation, take heart—funeral directors are here to help.

My personal experiences working with funeral directors in arranging my family members' services have all been incredibly positive, despite the emotional difficulty of making decisions while grieving. The funeral directors did everything possible to help me through the process by speaking slowly, answering the same question I had multiple times, and taking breaks when I needed to collect my thoughts and composure. As a pastor officiating services, I have also worked with many funeral homes and directors over the last twenty-plus years and have found all directors to be compassionate people who are aware of the difficulty you are experiencing.

There are two special contributors to this chapter: Ken Graham and Lon Dreyer, both funeral directors from funeral homes in Northern California (Fairfield and Napa, respectively). Ken co-authored this chapter, writing from his extensive experience as a funeral director and his personal desire to help families. Lon—a friend with whom I've collaborated to facilitate dozens of services and who is always willing to provide insight into his profession—has provided mentorship through several interviews. With the help of these two experienced funeral directors, we will walk you through a step-by-step approach to selecting a funeral home or mortuary.

Choosing a Funeral Home or Mortuary

(Ken) What is the difference between a funeral home and mortuary? Although the two provide similar services, a mortuary tends to focus more on the science or process of preparing the deceased. A funeral home, under the guidance of a funeral director, also provides the service of preparing the deceased, but in addition, it generally offers more services and options when considering the memorial or funeral service. Only you can make the decision about which will serve you best, based on your needs. For the sake of simplicity, I will use the term *funeral home* to include both funeral home and mortuary from this point forward. The steps required for selecting a funeral home are essentially the same for those planning pre-need and those planning at-need.

Research a Reputable Funeral Home

Research online reviews for each funeral home you are considering, but keep in mind that a negative review might be based on one person's unrealistic expectations. If you see multiple recent negative reviews, then take it to heart; otherwise, if the reviews are positive and credible, proceed with an interview.

Ask your friends, clergy, hospice, hospital, and city chaplain for recommendations and ask specific questions about why they recommend that funeral home or director.

> *A Note from Rick*
> *Do not be surprised if hospitals, hospices, churches, and city chaplains do not recommend one funeral home over another. To maintain a professional relationship with each venue in their area, they may choose to remain neutral and recommend you interview all or some of the funeral homes in the area. If this is the case, then how do you benefit from asking for opinions? By asking another question, such as, "If I were to choose such-and-such funeral home, would I be making a wise choice?" That way, they can reply diplomatically by saying, "Yes, that would be a very good choice," or "You may want to continue looking or interviewing other funeral homes." Remember, despite this being a highly emotional time in your life, doing your homework will help you have a positive experience that you will remember for years to come.*

Take a Tour

If you have the luxury of time, call the funeral home to make an appointment. Most funeral homes are busy throughout the week with services, so having an appointment will allow you the time needed for questions and answers. However, if you need information immediately, you can stop by a funeral home to pick up flyers on services provided and get a visual of the lobby, chapel, and amenities, which will help determine if you want to schedule a meeting with the funeral director.

When you call to make an appointment, if you know that only certain dates will work for your service, it is helpful to find out upfront if they can accommodate your desired timeframe. If they are unavailable, you can move on to another funeral home. However, do not completely rule out a funeral home over the phone simply because they cannot accommodate your desired service date(s). Why? Because you may end up going back to them if other funeral homes have the same schedule conflicts.

During your tour, bring another person with you to be a second set of eyes and to take notes. It is not uncommon to miss details when we are hurried or under stress. Consider the following questions as you evaluate the funeral home:

- How did you feel when you walked in? Were you greeted warmly and professionally?
- Is the funeral home clean? Be sure to look at everything!
- Does the funeral home have its own "preparation room" where they would prepare your loved one, or is that done at a different location? If it is the latter, there may be transportation fees.
- Is the chapel large enough to accommodate your needs for a funeral or memorial service?
- Are there adequate restroom facilities, and are they clean?
- Are there adequate parking spots available for your anticipated number of guests?
- Does the funeral home host receptions on-site, and at what capacity? What kitchen facilities are available?
- Is there music/video equipment available?
  - What size and how many monitor(s) do they have for pictures/videos?
  - What format do pictures/videos/music need to be in to be compatible with their equipment?
  - Will they do a test of their sound and video system so you can gauge the quality of each?
  - Is there a charge to use their equipment, and who will operate it?
- Is the cemetery in good condition? Ask to see the area(s) where "in-wall vaults" are located. An "in-wall vault" (casket or urn placed behind a wall) is different than a plot.

As you visit prospective funeral homes, make sure you are comfortable with the overall quality of the facility and confident with the expertise of the staff. If you have any doubts, then continue your search elsewhere. Remember, it is always possible to re-visit a funeral home later. Keep in mind that if you select a funeral home and then later decide to move to another, there will be a charge to transfer the deceased to the new location. Therefore, it is prudent to do your due diligence in finding the right establishment to meet your needs.

> *Rick's Story*
> *In the case of my dad, who had a stroke on a Sunday and passed away Monday morning, I had fewer than six hours to move him because the hospital didn't have a morgue. I only learned this upon his death; this is something I should have asked or been told while he was in the ED and ICU. Shock would be an understatement of how I felt with this news. This is also proof that while you are under stress, forgetting to ask pertinent questions is normal. It is common for a hospital to focus on healing the patient and providing hope for the family rather than on what happens afterward. If your loved one is in critical condition, be sure to ask in advance how much time you would have to move the deceased. This will dictate your sense of urgency and determine how much time you have, to interview funeral homes.*

Meet with the Funeral Director

As you are investigating your options, you will likely meet with one or more funeral directors at various locations to discuss the services they provide and the associated costs. How do you approach this subject? Be a student and learn as much as you can. If you interview multiple funeral homes, what you learn with each interview adds to your overall knowledge and ability to gain additional insight from each meeting.

Before your appointment, consider having a discussion with family members about the services you want and need. You can then offer your vision to the funeral director for a more focused conversation, but keep an open mind to the funeral director's full presentation. Choosing a funeral director you respect and trust will ease the stress on your family since he or she will be working with your family for days, weeks, or even months afterward.

Funeral Costs

When discussing costs with the funeral director, it's important to understand what the law says and what is *standard practice*. Ask for the general price list (GPL) and get a quote in writing for the service components you have chosen. Having a GPL is standard practice and could be the law in your state, as it is in California. The GPL is governed by and reviewed by the Cemetery and Funeral Bureau. Any prices listed on the funeral home website must match the prices quoted on paper. For more information on California's funeral laws, go to www.cfb.ca.gov. Or, research online for your state's governing laws and standard practices. Most funeral homes charge "Non-Declinable Services of Funeral Directors and Staff," also called "Professional Fees." Be sure to ask your funeral director what these fees cover.

Some funeral homes will offer direct burial or cremation packages. It is common to use a package as a promotional means to attract business. Every industry does it, and so do funeral homes. These packages can reduce the overall cost, *providing you are flexible and will work on their schedule*. This is a particularly good option if cost is a concern, but keep in mind that once you modify the package to fit your needs, the package deal could be negated, and your charges become itemized, resulting in a much greater cost. Be sure to shop and negotiate wisely.

Burial costs vary widely. After-death decisions, hopefully based on the deceased's wishes, will determine what services are needed from a funeral home and thus the cost incurred. These decisions are best made pre-need by the person planning in collaboration with his or her family. As hard as family or friends will work to "get it just right," having clear direction to follow as survivors is easier and less stressful. The choices you make regarding the following components will contribute to the final funeral home costs.

Burial vs. Cremation

If you choose burial, you will need to select a casket. Usually, a funeral home showroom has the corner pieces of caskets on display for selection. Both wood and metal caskets are available. Ask for costs on a pre-paid casket if you are pre-need. By pre-paying, the cost of your casket should not increase over time. If the casket you pre-purchased is no longer available at the time of death, it is customary to offer one of equal value as a substitute.

Burial involves costs related to the preparation of the deceased. This can include:
- Special care of autopsied remains.
- Preparation of the deceased for viewing of the un-embalmed body, including dressing, hairdressing, cosmetics, and casketing.
- Embalming.
- Refrigeration (typically billed by daily storage).
- Staff, facilities, and equipment cost.

If you choose cremation, you may still need embalming or refrigeration services based on the length of time between death and cremation. A rental casket can be used for the deceased for viewing during a service, if desired. The processing of cremated remains is a separate service from the actual cremation, so ask the funeral director for more information on this. Once the deceased is cremated, you will need an urn or other container approved for human remains. To reduce costs for burial or cremation, consider a cardboard container with a liner. If you choose to divide the cremated remains into multiple containers, it is necessary to purchase a permit for each vessel and state the location where each vessel will be stored.

Service

Many funeral homes provide a venue for funeral or memorial services. The size and type of service desired will determine your needs and expenses. Will your service be on a weekend or weekday? Will you have a catered reception? Will there be a viewing? (A viewing and service on the same day will save you money versus two separate days, which will require additional staff hours and facility use at additional costs.) Regardless of the type of service you decide upon, there is usually a two to three-day period that is required to obtain the necessary signatures from the doctor and permits before a service can take place. Check with your state or funeral home for exact time frames. On some occasions, though, if an immediate service is needed for religious purposes or preferences, a rush can be placed to obtain the necessary paperwork.

For more detailed information about planning a service, see chapter nine.

Burial Location

- *Burial plots* (in the ground) are controlled by the cemetery if separate from the funeral home. Cost varies based on location within the cemetery.
- An *in-wall vault* is when a casket or urn is placed behind a wall.
- *Crypt vaults* are stone chambers in cemeteries or beneath churches and other religious buildings, or occasionally beneath chapels or mausoleums on personal property. They are not as popular today in the United States as in the past. There is no requirement that embalming be performed unless an indoor crypt burial occurs, and the cemetery has policy requirements for such.

- A *columbarium* is a wall with recessed areas for the interment of urns containing the ashes of the deceased.
- *Mausoleums* are large, architecturally beautiful buildings with multiple tombs to house the deceased in caskets.

Often you may hear someone say, "When I'm gone, it doesn't matter." There may be truth in that statement for the deceased, but not always for the survivors. Plan with your family in mind. When you choose a cemetery, consider others who will want to visit your gravesite or place of interment in the future. Will it be too far for family and friends to visit? This could impact the frequency of visitation, which may be important to you or them. Also consider the aesthetics of the cemetery. Is this a location where you would like family and friends to visit in the future? I (Rick) have been to many cemeteries that are incredibly old but beautiful. Likewise, I have been to cemeteries that are much newer yet show signs of age far beyond what they should. This is a result of each cemetery choosing how they maintain their property, which quite often equates to their pride as an organization and cost—your cost.

Spreading Ashes

You may hear people say, "We spread the ashes ourselves in the mountains or at the beach," but that does not make it legal. Spreading ashes on land or water is governed by law, so learn about your own state's laws online or from your local funeral home.

A popular choice is burial-at-sea. If you are choosing burial-at-sea, the number of people attending is limited by boat capacity. The Neptune Society (www.neptunesociety.com) and other individuals and organizations offer licensed boats that can accommodate approximately six to twenty people. Some funeral homes also offer this service as part of their packages. Before my (Rick's) mom and dad reached their end-of-life, they purchased a package from a local funeral home. After my mom died, her ashes were held in storage for several months, waiting for the funeral home staff to spread her ashes at sea. My dad was under the impression we could participate in this sacred moment, but sadly, that was not the case since the funeral home used their private licensed boat that did not allow passengers. My dad was unwilling to deviate from the plan he and my mom had made, so her ashes were scattered without us. Later, however, he wished he had been able to participate in her final farewell.

After the death of my wife, Susie, and later my dad, I chartered a private boat operating out of Bodega Bay to spread their ashes. In each case, five family members and/or friends were able to accompany me. Susie, with her Texan humor, used to say, "When I go, just put me in a bag and throw me over the fence! Don't spend a lot of money burying me." But she was serious when she said, "I hope a salmon jumps out of the water into the boat as you are pouring my ashes." Well, wouldn't you know it, a salmon did jump out of the water awfully close to the boat when our family began pouring her ashes into the water! A few weeks after the small, private service to spread her ashes, we held a large memorial service with music and guest speakers.

For my dad, who was a veteran of the Royal Canadian Navy in World War II, we played the Canadian national anthem and a rendition of "Taps" recorded in a joint effort by the Canadian and American military bands as we placed his remains in the water. We followed with red and white rose petals sprinkled on the water, signifying the Canadian flag. Within a minute, the biodegradable heart-shaped urn did exactly what it was designed to do: It dropped about a foot under the surface—still visible—then after a few minutes, started to sink until it was out of sight. The slow descent brought a calmness and respect that surprised me, compared to the sudden drop from the stern of the boat that would have felt abrupt and cold—at least to me. "Farewell, Dad," I said. "You've been the best father imaginable. I'll see you again one day."

Headstones & Markers

What kind of marker will be used? The cost of an upright headstone or flat marker with your loved one's name, date of birth, and death varies based on material, size, and engraving. Funeral homes will assist you with finding a local business that supplies markers if they do not offer this service.

Transportation

If the deceased undergoes an autopsy and requires transportation from the place of death to the coroner's office, there could be a cost incurred. One set fee covers this, unless the cause of death was homicide or the deceased was an infant, in which cases the fee is waived (check your county and state for accuracy). Once a body is released by the coroner's office, there is a short grace period for the deceased to be moved to a funeral home. After notice has been given to move the deceased, and the grace period has expired for removal, a daily storage fee can be charged (see chapter five "Struggling with Sudden Death" for more information on the coroner's office).

Another instance in which you might face transportation costs is if you have a funeral or memorial service in a location separate from the cemetery. Having both a chapel and cemetery on the same property decreases the cost for transportation of the deceased and increases the percentage of attendance by family and friends should you have both a funeral and a graveside service.

Laws vary when it comes to transporting the deceased to another city, state, or country, and the cost elevates quickly. For California, it is not unusual for the family to pay three dollars per mile after thirty miles for transportation. Transporting a casket from one funeral home to another out-of-state funeral home requires a "burial permit" and a release form from the family. Transporting cremated remains out of state requires a "disposition permit." This permit is also required to spread the ashes at sea.

Required Information for the Funeral Director

Once you have decided on a funeral home and the services you need, you will need to provide them with the necessary administrative details.

Death Certificate Data

The funeral home typically provides death certificates. Collect and submit the following information to your funeral director:
- Full legal name of the deceased: first, middle, last.
- Gender.
- Full residence address, city, state, and zip code.
- City and state or foreign country of birth.
- Date of birth (month, day, and year).
- Age.
- Date of death.
- Place of death.
- Cause of death.
- Social Security number (keep this in a secure location).
- Veteran's discharge or claim number (DD214 form).
- Marital status.
- Ethnicity.
- Occupation.
- Highest level of education.
- Next of kin.
- Holder of the Power of Attorney (POA) or Durable Power of Attorney (DPOA). The definition of this can vary from state to state, so research this online or with your attorney.

How many death certificates you need will vary based on several factors, but the average number ordered ranges from five to twenty. Why is there such a variance? Estate size and complexity is one reason. When closing accounts or filing a claim, ask if an original death certificate is required or if a copy will be sufficient. Sending a copy will save you money. Generally, death certificates are needed for changes or claims made to:
- Insurance companies.
- Bank accounts.
- Brokerage accounts.
- Credit card companies.
- Employer HR department.
- Social Security Administration.
- Retirement plans.

- Deed on home/property.
- Auto/DMV.

Authorizations

From the answers and information provided on the death certificate worksheet, the following documents will be generated for the family to sign:

- A release form allowing the mortuary to keep the deceased in their care until the requested services are performed.
- An embalming authorization form, stating whether embalming is requested or declined.
- A cremation authorization document if cremation is desired and a form for the disposition of the cremated remains.
- A disclosure document from the mortuary, stating whether the mortuary/funeral home has prepaid funding set aside for funeral services.

Obituary Information

Your funeral home of choice can either write or help you write an obituary for your loved one. Publishing an obituary in the local newspaper can be expensive. Most funeral homes have websites and will offer to list your loved one's obituary and space to leave notes for survivors at no charge. This is not meant to replace any legal purposes for posting an obituary in the newspaper and may not satisfy any legal requirements, so please check with your legal representative for more information.

To prepare an obituary, obtain the following information for the funeral director or author:

- Full legal name of the deceased: first, middle, last.
- Other names went by (AKA).
- Date of birth (month, day, and year).
- Age.
- City and state or foreign country of birth.
- Armed Forces service.

- Marital status.
- Ethnicity.
- Occupation(s) (include dates and employers and number of years in occupation).
- Residence: city and state.
- Year moved to the county of residence.
- Name of spouse (if married).
- Father's first, middle, and last name.
- Father's birth state or country.
- Mother's first, middle, last (maiden name).
- Mother's birth state or country.
- Names of family members – relationship – city and state of residence.
- Cities where he or she lived and when he or she lived there.
- Organization(s) of which he or she had been a member, including offices held.
- Interests, hobbies, talents, awards, and community activities.
- Outstanding work.
- Education/college degrees.
- Give time and place of funeral/memorial.
- Charities for memorial contributions.
- Religious affiliation.

Action Steps

- If your loved one has received a critical diagnosis and the medical professional has discussed the possibility of death, call your hospital or provider to ask if the hospital has a morgue and how much time you will have before the deceased needs to be moved.
- Research funeral homes online and become familiar with terminology, services, and prices in your area. Talk with friends, clergy, hospitals, hospice, or city chaplains for their recommendations.
- If you or your loved one has life insurance or a burial policy, review it for the policy amount, which will help you determine the services you can afford.
- Begin compiling the paperwork needed by the funeral home.

CHAPTER 9

Planning a Funeral or Memorial Service

I officiated a service recently at Sacramento Valley National Cemetery. Since the deceased was a veteran of the United States Air Force, two uniformed service members were present to play "Taps" and perform the flag folding and presentation to the surviving spouse. As the hearse approached, the airmen, decorated with ribbons on their chests and stripes on their sleeves, came to attention and saluted. While the family entered the shelter, one airman remained outside preparing to play "Taps," and the other walked in and stood at attention. "Taps" played from a distance in that slow cadence undeniably consumes your senses; it is emotional and commanding. After they folded the flag with absolute precision and honored the deceased with a three-second salute, one airman knelt and presented the flag to the surviving spouse. "On behalf of the President of the United States, the United States Air Force, and a grateful nation, please accept this flag as a symbol of our appreciation for your loved one's honorable and faithful service."

After his presentation of the flag, he stood at attention, saluted, and then turned with an intentional sliding of his heel on the cement, creating a scratching sound from his metal heel plate and a steady click from his heels as he slowly exited. Perfection! Did it make an impact? Absolutely. Then I followed with my message, which is never easy after you witness active military honoring a veteran. After the service, I spoke with the veteran's spouse, who expressed her joy to see her husband honored by the United States Air Force and with a message that was personal, accurate, and healing. For her, this was perfection.

Will the funeral/memorial service you plan be perfect? Will it be like the active military members of the Old Guard at Arlington National Cemetery, who spend hours every night preparing for the following day to honor the fallen and veterans? Probably not because it is not a realistic expectation to compare a civilian service with the elite crew of the Old Guard. But with thoughtful planning, you, too, can prepare an honorable and gratifying service.

Types of Services

As a pastor and officiant, I've had survivors tell me, "I would rather you plan my service because I don't know how to do it." The goal of this chapter is to equip you to plan a service, whether pre-need or at-need, or to serve as an officiant for your family member or friend's service. Knowledge is empowering!

People have also asked me, "What will happen if I don't have a service? Will people be upset with me? Is a service necessary?" I asked myself the same question in the case of my dad, who at ninety-one years of age had dementia and very few friends still alive. In my experience, not having a service is like not finishing a good book or movie; it ends abruptly and without completion. Having a service of some design allows you to recognize a date, time, and location where you came together—regardless of the size of group—to honor your loved one. Having a service is part of the closure process. Closure, in this case, is not to forget your loved one, but rather, to honor your loved one and remember what is important. A service should be—in my opinion—part of your loved one's legacy.

Planning a service is very much like planning a wedding, and it can be as simple or elaborate as you choose.

Chapel-Only Service with or without a Reception

Whether you use a funeral home's chapel, cemetery, church, synagogue, temple, or another place of worship for a service, you must decide if this concludes the service or if the family—and maybe guests—will then leave for a graveside service. The primary benefit of a chapel-only service is that attendees need only drive to one location versus driving to a second location for a graveside service. Transportation of flowers and memorabilia from the chapel, church, synagogue, temple, or another place of worship to the cemetery for a graveside service is also eliminated, which will reduce the amount of work and planning required.

If the facility you choose has a designated space for a reception, then the reception immediately following a funeral/memorial will typically be well-attended. If the reception is off-site, then people find it easier to excuse themselves, which will reduce participation.

Chapel and Graveside Service

Having both a chapel and graveside service does not mean everyone is invited to the gravesite. This is a choice that families make days or weeks prior to the chapel service and can be announced by the officiant or included in the program for attendees. My experience has been that for grieving families who want to spend time alone at the gravesite after the service, this is a sacred and intimate time. It's also important to note that many cemeteries prefer you do not stay for the burial of the casket and covering of the grave. But, in all cases, you are invited to return hours later or in the ensuing days to visit. This is both done for safety since heavy equipment will be operating and because, for most families, it is hard to see their loved one lowered into the ground.

Chapel and Graveside Service with Reception to Follow

If there is a graveside service immediately after the funeral/memorial and guests are invited, the typical percentage of people attending the graveside service will be about 25 percent. The average attendance for people attending the reception without going to the graveside service will be about 50–75 percent of the people who attended the chapel service.

Service Components

Whenever I meet with a family to plan a service, I ask them, "What do you want guests to see and hear at your service?" These priorities will determine which elements you include in a service, which affect its flow. People will always remember the service components that did not work/flow together, but when a service is done well, it is seamless, and attendees' memories are uninterrupted by avoidable mistakes. Appendix B at the back of this book has sample "Order of Service Templates" for you to use. The following are common components of funeral or memorial services.

Prayer

Depending upon your personal convictions (faith and beliefs) or those of your loved one, you may choose to include prayer at both the opening of the service and conclusion. If you are not a person of faith but choose to have prayer as a service component, then consider asking a family member or friend of faith to offer this part of the service. Having others participate helps the service to be more inclusive.

Music

Music can set the tone for your service. Select music that you identify with and that is appropriate for the people attending. The number of songs you choose will impact the length of service, and where you insert the songs in the order of service will affect the flow. I encourage you to consider having two to four songs played before the service begins as people view the memorabilia and find their seats. This serves as a calming presence for people during a potentially difficult time.

Discuss with your funeral director the logistics required to arrange pre-recorded or live music. If the music will be pre-recorded, ask the funeral director how he or she would like it provided. Will the funeral director download the music from a website, or will you supply it on a USB drive or CD? If you are supplying the music, offer it to the funeral director at least two days prior to the service to be sure your choice of technology is compatible with his or her equipment. It is extremely frustrating for both family, officiant, and the funeral director when the music or other media fail to play because of incompatibility with technology. If you will be having live music in the service, confirm with the funeral director and your musicians what equipment will be provided by the venue and who will manage the soundboard.

Media

If you choose to have a video or slideshow of pictures on the screen, consider the length of time this takes from the service. Just like music, each portion of the service should be timed and inserted to assist in the flow. One idea for the slideshow is to play it on a loop before and after the service. Videos, on the other hand, should be played during or at the end of service since they require active attention by the attendees. Like pre-recorded music, make sure to deliver the video(s) to your funeral director ahead of time and in the correct format. Before the service begins, check to make sure that the video or slideshow will display properly.

Memorabilia

It is common to have pictures of your loved one in the lobby or by the casket/urn. These pictures range from older small pictures pinned on a board to larger framed photos that stand on easels. If there is a part of your or your loved one's life you want to high-light, such as medals from military service, vocational awards, or personal art or hobby items, these can be displayed too. Just remember, a little says a lot. Moderation is your friend here.

Guest Speaker(s) & Open Mic Time

Not everyone should be a guest speaker, but the right person can be highly effective. My suggestion here is simple: Ask individuals who will stay within a time frame, speak honorably about the deceased, and offer varying perspectives. For example, if everyone speaking is from the deceased's workplace, then that offers only one perspective. But, if you choose people from different parts of the deceased's life—family members, friends, colleagues, school friends, and so on—each will offer a different perspective. How many guest speakers are enough? That varies, depending upon the focus and planned length of the service. Well-chosen guest speakers will be able to share accurate and personal stories about the deceased's life that flow well with what the officiant shares.

An open-mic time, allowing anyone to share from where they are seated or by coming to the pulpit, can be very honoring but should be introduced and managed by the officiant. If you are aware of someone in attendance who may be inappropriate with their sharing, alert the officiant in advance so they can be on guard to minimize the impact and spare the family embarrassment. There's nothing so memorable as having to take the microphone away and cut someone off. To avoid this possibility, you may choose not to include an open-mic time in the service at all.

Flowers

Flowers have the unique ability to soften the look and feel of the service, which is comforting. But flowers also have scents that some people are allergic to, so keep this in mind when selecting flowers. In addition, like memorabilia, a little can go a long way, so consider space available and the quantity of flowers you desire. Also, flowers are normally moved to the gravesite if there is a graveside service afterward, so think about transportation.

Donations to Charity

It is common today for the surviving family to ask for donations to designated charitable organizations in honor of the deceased. This is a personal choice and should be promoted if the deceased had expressed this desire. If the family has made that decision after the death of their loved one, then serious consideration should be given to what the deceased would have chosen, thus eliminating any perception of impropriety by directing funds elsewhere.

Research the organization named as a potential recipient and collect the following information:

- Organization's name.
- Address.
- Mission.
- How to give (online, check, in-person, etc.).
- EIN (Employer Identification Number) for tax-deduction purposes.

Providing credible information will increase the benevolence of the giving community.

Viewing

Viewing your loved one is optional. This is a choice made either ahead of time through planning with the funeral director or by the surviving family or friend managing the deceased's affairs. Viewing your loved one is typically done before the funeral (normally by invitation, so you control who will be in attendance). If you choose to have an open-casket service, anyone in attendance will be able to view the deceased before the casket is closed. Keep in mind that a viewing should take into consideration the cause of death and appearance. Even though most funeral homes do excellent work to make the deceased look their best, there are times when the cause of death may leave a person disfigured. In such cases, choosing not to have a viewing allows the lasting memory to be more honoring to the deceased.

The Officiant

The term "officiant," which is most often associated with clergy, describes the person who will officiate a service. In layman terms, some might call the officiant an emcee or master of ceremonies. I would describe an officiant as "a person whose role is to lead a formal service, such as a burial, marriage, baby dedication, baptism, or other religious event." These individuals are usually vocational clergy ordained by their denomination or faith affiliation. In addition, chaplains, who are usually associated with institutions, such as hospitals, law enforcement, military, fire departments, or large corporations that provide faith-based counseling or access to a person of faith also perform these sacerdotal duties. Contrary to vocational clergy, not all officiants are ordained; some may be "serving" in that role for their house of worship or denomination, fulfilling a ministry as trained volunteers.

Choosing an Officiant

Choosing an officiant for your service is an extremely personal decision. If planning your service pre-need, you have the option of interviewing clergy and selecting one with whom you feel comfortable. If the deceased had not made plans, and arrangements are being made at the time of death, then choosing an officiant can be challenging because it is such a personal decision to make with short notice.

If you are a person of faith, a good choice is to first contact the house of worship the deceased called home. Since different faiths have different views of death and burial, it is critical—if you want to follow the doctrine of the person's faith—to start where he or she attended. This is especially important if the deceased had planned for end-of-life, naming a house of worship and officiant as the venue and clergy for the service. Connecting with that religious leader will afford you quick answers to questions and an officiant accustomed to his or her beliefs and venue at little or no charge.

If you or the deceased do not have a history of faith or are not active in a house of worship, then finding an officiant through the funeral home or mortuary you choose or a city chaplain through your local law enforcement agency or fire department are excellent options. The funeral home will immediately start calling its list of officiants that best match the deceased's personal beliefs. A personal note here—as a pastor, when I am contacted about officiating a service for someone who was not a person of faith, I'm okay with that—in fact, I welcome it. About 95 percent of the funerals/memorials I officiate outside of the church are for people who identify as not having a religious faith connected to a recognized mainstream religion. Personally, I love to get these calls because it gives me an opportunity to meet people outside of the church and serve them, and hopefully provide them with a positive experience with a person of faith. If you are not a person of faith and you connect with a pastor, minister, priest, rabbi, and so on, try to foster a friendship with the officiant because he or she could be of tremendous value in helping you through your grief and connecting you with available resources.

Is a family member or friend a good choice to be the officiant? In most cases, probably not. I recall meeting with a family member days ahead of a memorial service. She wanted to be "the" guest speaker for the family but admitted that it would be difficult to fight through the emotions and anticipated tears. I assured her that speaking for one to two minutes only after writing down her thoughts and practicing would help. On the day of the service, we connected for a minute as people were gathering so I could encourage her. "I am ready," she responded. *Great, here we go!* I thought. As the service progressed nicely and her time arrived, she approached the podium with notes in hand, with what appeared to be a great confidence. I was ready to hear her story. She took a deep breath, paused, then took another deep breath, followed by another pause, and then her face started turning red, and tears burst like a winter rain. Five minutes later, despite my offer to help, she sat down, having never said a word. Was this her fault? No, absolutely not! She did the best she was capable of at the time. But it is a good reminder that when someone has a substantial emotional tie to the deceased, this could, and does, happen.

An experienced clergy or ministry leader trained to officiate services can be invaluable compared to someone untrained and the learning curve he or she will face. Think about where you work and what you do. Can someone walk in and with a few minutes of training do your job, under pressure, and hopefully do it better than you? I seriously doubt it, but that is the expectation of someone untrained. It is unrealistic in most cases, and not fair to the person officiating or to the deceased. These are decisions that should be made well in advance, offering the layperson a chance to prepare. Should you choose to take this path of assigning a family member or friend as the officiant, then refer to the Order of Service Templates in the back of this book and the resources available on this book's website (www.WhenItsTime.org). Documents, such as the Family Questionnaire© and sample messages, will assist the untrained officiant.

Whomever you choose to officiate the service, keep in mind that if you have more than one service (such as chapel and graveside), you will need an officiant for both. If the services are in locations that are distant from each other, you may need two different officiants.

Emotions play a significant role in decision-making, and it's important to make a connection with your chosen officiant that leaves you feeling comfortable and confident. To achieve this, interview the potential officiant about his or her capabilities and experience with officiating funerals and memorials. Questions you could ask include:

- How long have you been involved in this ministry?
- How many services have you officiated?
- How important is it to you to collect information about the deceased, and how do you go about that?
- What does a typical order of service look like for you?
- Do you recommend guest speakers or open mic time, and how does that affect your time speaking? If he or she pushes back on guest speakers taking too much of "his or her" time, consider looking for a different officiant. Why? Because designing a service could/should include

guest speakers or open mic time, in addition to the officiant sharing his or her message.

• What is the recommended service time? This will vary with a house of worship, but if you listen closely to "why" the officiant is recommending one order of service over another, the focal point should always be to promote a flow that will honor the family and take into consideration the amount of time people are sitting. Whether you are a young child or an elderly person, sitting for long periods of time can be uncomfortable, so the officiant should explain this to the survivors and be flexible to meet the need.

If the interview process is incomplete or expectations are not explored thoroughly, you may politely explain that you don't feel comfortable with the process and either start over with trying to understand his or her position or share that you feel more comfortable finding another officiant. Do not be shy about making this call, but be respectful because you may circle back to this officiant if you cannot locate another.

Officiant Expectations and Preparation

Your expectations and the officiant's preparation should be thoroughly explored to arrive at a mutual understanding of what a "win" would look and sound like on the day of the service(s).

Anything short of a shared vision and understanding could result in expectations not being met, and hence, the family not feeling like closure has begun. Unmet expectations make it easy to focus on what "did not" happen during the service or the mistakes that were made. What goes wrong is what you will remember.

It's the officiant's responsibility to ask questions—and a lot of them—to minimize mistakes and increase a favorable outcome. When securing an officiant for my brother's funeral, I contacted

Rob's church for a discussion about having a pastor officiate the service. I received a call back immediately from a pastor, and during this brief conversation on the phone, I could sense this would be our only conversation prior to his funeral if I didn't take action. Knowing that without personal information, the service would be more liturgical (reading of Scripture and other denominational customs), which was not what our family was desiring, so I requested a meeting to discuss Rob's legacy. Reluctantly, the pastor agreed to a lunch meeting. As we had lunch and talked, I told stories about Rob, which included an in-depth discourse about his military experience, of which he was extremely proud. At no time during our lunch did the pastor take notes. This should have been a red flag, but I said nothing, trusting he was accomplished in pastoral care.

At the funeral, the Riverside Sheriff's Department was in attendance since Rob was a badge-carrying volunteer sheriff, along with members of the United States Army to honor one of their own. As the service progressed, some of the stories the pastor shared about Rob were incorrect, and even more disappointing, he tried to make a joke about a mission Rob had participated in looking for POWs after the Vietnam War ended. I had told him the full story at our lunch meeting, but without notes or proper preparation, his message felt dishonoring to my brother's legacy. At the end of the service, he asked if anyone would like to say anything about Rob, so I addressed those in attendance, thanking them for honoring Rob with their presence, and shared a few accurate stories.

Unfortunately, despite the officiant at my brother's funeral being an ordained clergy member—and he may be excellent at other parts of his ministry, which I respect—he lacked the experience to officiate Rob's service well. So, what I remember most about his funeral at Riverside National Cemetery is what went wrong at the service, which hindered me from taking the next step in closure. This could have been avoided by employing a more thorough interview process.

Each officiant will have his or her own methodology of how to gain information, so let me share how I work by way of example. Once I receive the call from a funeral home or a direct call from the family, I set an appointment with them as soon as possible. I also email the Family Questionnaire© I developed so they can start working on it ahead of time and return the document before our meeting. During our initial phone conversation, I confirm service details, such as date, time, location, and some background information on the deceased. I also ask for information, such as military branch and rank, places of deployment, special assignments, service with law enforcement/fire department, and positions held at public companies and community organizations. Then I begin my homework, researching these areas for background knowledge even before I receive the Family Questionnaire©. Keep in mind, if it is a funeral, the officiant only has about three to ten days to prepare. This is not much time since most officiants' schedules are full.

Between my research and the Family Questionnaire©, I already have a good sense of the deceased by the time I meet with the family in-person (if possible). During our appointment, we review the Family Questionnaire©, and I ask more questions to get to know their loved one better. If I didn't know him or her personally, I must gain enough information to deliver a message that is personal and has some degree of passion. I ask questions to gain a sense of the person's personality, hobbies, education, vocation, interest in outdoor activities, achievements, political views, cultural differences, family members and dynamics, favorite movies/plays, religious background, favorite Bible verses, taste in music, and so on. Like a professional photographer who snaps 500–1,000 pictures but only uses a few, so it is with the officiant when crafting his or her message. Personally, I do not use a notebook/laptop to take notes during the family meeting. I find it distracting and not engaging, which could translate into not making a connection. Instead, I write on the Family Questionnaire© while keeping eye contact as much as possible and practicing reflective listening.

These questions can be painful for the survivors to talk about, but many also find it to be a therapeutic release for their emotions and perhaps even a chance to finally divulge those family secrets to a safe person. So, as an officiant, I dig deep, but am also mindful and respectful that I'm sitting with people who are grieving. A good officiant takes his or her time and operates under the umbrella of grace, love, and confidentiality. To help experience closure, the family needs to talk, share stories, laugh, cry, weep, and then laugh again as they tell more stories, helping them remember the best about their loved one and their loved one's legacy. The role the officiant plays is crucial in helping the family heal.

Once I meet with the family, I pray for guidance and begin crafting a message that will hopefully honor the family and the deceased. Several renditions will happen as new information comes in, guest speakers are added or removed, or the order of service is changed to adapt for various components. Even once my final message is ready, it can and often does change minutes before the service begins.

After the Service

If there is a reception at the funeral home or church following the service, I attend for a short time to connect with people. I have found they are open to talking about the deceased and their personal experiences with him or her, the family, and how they liked or did not like the service. Conversations can range from seeking help for how to grieve, requesting counselors' names and numbers, asking for guidance for their own family members who are ill, or making a general statement about the service; all input is appreciated and received. If the reception is at the person's home, I generally do not attend for a couple of reasons: my own time limitations and because when the family is in their home, they are busy serving others, and I feel my presence is more of a hindrance than a benefit. Instead, I follow up and connect at a later date.

Once the service and reception are finished, I go home and reflect upon the day and ask myself three questions: What was good, what should I do differently, and what did I learn? I never stop learning, so I never stop asking these questions.

Honorariums

What does it cost to have an officiant perform a funeral/memorial/graveside service? This depends upon what the person is being asked to perform, geographical location, and his or her religious affiliation. Most officiants receive an honorarium, which is a dollar amount given as a thank-you gift. Generally speaking, if the officiant is asked to serve the family with a funeral/memorial only, then $300–$400 is normal. If the officiant is asked to provide both a message for the funeral and graveside, then $350–$450 is normal. This is the norm for where I live in California, so ask your funeral director or officiant directly for input about the average honorarium in your area.

It is not uncommon for a person who is a member of a church or religious organization to not give an honorarium to the officiant because the pastor, minister, priest, rabbi, or other religious leader is a "vocational leader." However, keep in mind that to not honor the officiant with a gift can also communicate that you expect them to "just do his or her job," when his or her profession may already require them to work fifty to sixty hours per week at a forty-hour-per-week compensation level. Honorariums allow you to acknowledge the effort that an officiant puts into preparing for a service.

Action Steps

- Begin planning your or your loved one's service. Include family members and friends in the process to discuss logistics, delegate service components, and find out if they wish to visit the gravesite later.
- Contact your venue of choice to inquire about available dates, packages, and cost of a service.
- Interview potential officiants. If you are considering having a family or friend officiate your service, provide them with the Family Questionnaire© and Order of Service Templates (available at www.WhenItsTime.org) and share your expectations.
- Research charitable organizations and gather the information needed for donations.

CHAPTER 10

Understanding Your Health Insurance

W hen my wife, Susie, died, I was fully expecting our medical insurance company to continue her coverage with final
billing and payment up to death and related post-death charges.
Susie's body gave out about thirty-six hours after entering the
hospital. I was not prepared for her health insurance company to
do the same.

Upon her death, our insurance company stopped paying all
related costs for both her stay in the hospital and up to one month
prior to end-of-life. The bills continued to arrive for weeks, and
the dollar amount I was responsible for continued to grow. I understood that medical bills took time to process, but this was radically
different—they were being rejected altogether.

Overwhelmed by medical bills and the legal work I needed to
complete, I eventually asked the hospital for a case manager and
her insurance company for a representative to sort through the
confusion. After weeks of auditing by the hospital, her insurance
company, and myself, they finally arrived at an agreed billable
amount, and the hospital resubmitted the bills to the insurance
company. My portion of the bill was reduced by tens of thousands of dollars to $3,000–$4,000 out-of-pocket. Was the hospital or insurance company at fault for over-billing, or was this a
case of too many moving parts to track properly? I honestly don't

know, but I learned that the adage, "measure twice and cut once" is a reality!

So, how do you work with hospitals and insurance companies at an end-of-life event? Slowly is my advice! Inspect everything. But are you the best person to do so? Only you can answer that question, but I can assure you, if you ask for help from family members and trusted friends, that extra set of eyes and reasoning will not only give you confidence the billing/payment you make is correct, but it will also ease the burden.

Lending her expert advice on this topic is independent insurance agent Timothea "TJ" Galoner, who also happens to be a friend of mine from high school. We will combine my personal experience and her expertise in plans, carriers, and industry terminology throughout this chapter to give you detailed insight to help minimize your stress and financial challenges.

Understanding Your Health Insurance Plan

"Prepare, practice, and execute" is a mode of operation used by first responders, military, and industries involving potentially dangerous environmental disasters. So, what can the layperson learn from this? The same theory applies, to some degree, for end-of-life preparation when considering your medical insurance coverage, medical facilities available to you, and current and anticipated medical needs, which includes chronic illnesses. Taking the first step to prepare is essential if you want to minimize stress—emotionally, physically, and financially. Start today because it will be a gift to you and your loved ones later!

Finding a knowledgeable health insurance agent can bring you clarity about your benefits and keep you from the potentially devastating pitfall of not understanding your health plan. Health policies can be complicated instruments, so do not be shy about asking questions. Again, I (TJ) suggest having a trusted person with you who can process clearly, take notes, and advise you based on information gathered.

PPO vs. HMO

The main difference between an PPO and an HMO is in flexibility to choose your provider. If your health plan is a Preferred Provider Organization (PPO), it should allow you to choose a hospital rather than being assigned a hospital. Remember, however, that even PPOs work within specific networks. If you go outside that network, your cost will be higher than if you use hospitals within the network.

A health maintenance organization (HMO) is just that: They *maintain* your plan of care through a primary care physician (PCP), who decides which specialist you should see for "continuity of care." In this case, you cannot self-refer to a specialist, and even if the PCP has referred you to a specialist or for a special procedure, the medical group your plan is under can veto that decision. If they have several locations, you may get the "feel" of being able to choose where to go; however, if you seek medical attention outside of their network and they do not deem it to be an emergency, there is a high probability you will be 100 percent responsible for the bill.

Out-of-Network Providers

If the patient was taken to a hospital "out-of-network," call your carrier (medical insurance company) and *alert them immediately*. Explain to the carrier that your loved one is at a hospital out-of-network and request authorization for treatment until that person can be moved or reaches end-of-life. Failure to do so could allow the carrier to be selective on what charges they will cover, leaving you or the deceased's estate financially responsible for the remainder of the bill. As an example, a friend of mine (Rick's) (who had an HMO) took his son to an out-of-network hospital close to his home when he broke his arm. This seemed reasonable since his arm was noticeably broken, and he was in extreme pain. But when my friend was billed by his carrier, it was for the entire bill: emergency room visit, doctor's fees, medication, cast for his son's arm, and so on. Why? Because the medical group reviewing his case determined it was not a situation where he needed emergency treatment. They stood firm, saying he could have driven the extra ten to twelve miles to the local hospital in the HMO's network, so he was responsible for 100 percent of the bill, as stated in his plan. It was an expensive lesson to learn. The story should not have ended there because he could have—and probably should have—appealed the decision. But like so many of us, he did not fully understand his plan and did not pursue financial recovery by appealing the decision. What you do not know can hurt you. What you do know empowers you!

Deductibles

Check with your insurance company for deductibles involving hospital stays and medication while your loved one is a patient. Why? Because some insurance plans have extremely high deductibles, so it is important to know this going in rather than being surprised later. In addition, check for deductibles on home health care and equipment if released to your home for extended care to minimize surprises.

Choosing a Plan and Provider

Planning pre-need and at-need can be vastly different when it comes to end-of-life in a hospital or medical facility. I (Rick) have experienced both. Personally, I failed to do my homework ahead of Susie's death; therefore, my wife's end-of-life left me consumed working with her PPO on billing and the additional emotional challenges that ensued. When my dad had a massive stroke, he was taken to the closest hospital, which was out-of-network since his insurance plan was an HMO. I had learned my lesson through my wife's death, so I managed his experience differently as a result.

Planning pre-need gives you the flexibility to choose an insurance plan and healthcare provider that will cover your end-of-life needs adequately. When choosing a plan or provider, consider some of the following areas:

- Does the hospital network covered by your plan have the level of medical treatment available that you might need? Keep in mind that a rural hospital, for example, may not have the ability to treat certain medical conditions.
- Does the healthcare plan cover specialty equipment and services, such as physical therapy, which often requires both equipment and personnel?
- Does the provider have trained staff for home health care, and at what cost? Does your plan cover hospice and palliative care?
- Does the provider waive fees post-end-of-life? Do they offer payment plans? What financial assistance is available?
- Do I qualify for a subsidized plan or other benefit programs based on my income level?

Hospitals often receive donations to the main entity or to departments as they expand. If you or your loved one is interested in giving to their cause or vision, this may be a consideration in choosing one hospital or medical facility over another.

If you are planning at-need after your loved one has experienced end-of-life in a hospital or medical facility, you'll still need to explore the topics listed above. But instead of choosing a health plan in advance to procure the desired hospital/medical facility and benefits, you will be forced to maneuver within the patient's existing health plan, negotiating where possible.

If end-of-life does not include proven treatments, then consider investigating prescription medicine used in "studies," which could come at a reduced charge or no charge. Having an in-depth conversation with your medical professional should offer insight into this often confusing but evolving industry.

Getting Organized

Hospital and medical bills, in general, can be very confusing—
and that is an understatement! Compound that with grieving and
the legal work that demands your attention, and inaccuracies will
inevitably be overlooked. So, here are some suggestions for a
system to help you.

While your loved one is in the hospital, hospice, or rehabil-
itation facility, keep a spiral notebook labeled "patient journal."
Designate a leader—in shifts—who will journal all activity, such
as medical personnel visitation and their purpose, medication
given, protocol changes, and so on. This helps inform the next shift
of visiting family members or friends of events and changes. This
tool also becomes invaluable when reviewing future bills. Keep
all bills and related medical paperwork in a folder or binder in
chronological order. In addition, keep any notes you have taken in
chronological order so you can compare your daily notes with the
billing dates. This is where the patient journal becomes invaluable.

If possible, accumulate all important paperwork needed like
DNRs, DPOA, insurance policy numbers, Medicare/Medicaid
information, and so on into one place, separated by tabs or sticky
notes for easy reference. If you have not been a user of the medical
facility chosen, then typically, they will *not* receive your paperwork until admitted, so having them in your file will save time
and emotional energy. You will appreciate how much easier it is
to find that important document you need *right now!*

Billing

After all the hospital bills I (Rick) received—and there were
dozens—my smartest move was to ask for a case manager, who
is sometimes called an "administrative liaison," from the hospital,
who worked with a health insurance representative. Together, they
eventually agreed to a total dollar amount concerning my wife's
medical bills. This lowered—as I mentioned at the beginning of
this chapter—my final bill by tens of thousands of dollars. In retrospect, I should have had a trusted friend go through all the bills

with me as an extra set of eyes to minimize my time invested. The big lesson here: Get help! Build your team!

The deceased's estate—if managed by someone who acts as the durable power of attorney (DPOA) or trustee—will have to contact the insurance carrier to inform them of the death and manage the billing process. If no recognized person has been assigned, then the "next of kin" holding a valid death certificate can represent the estate of the deceased.

Applying for Assistance

If, after receiving the final bill(s), you find you are not capable of paying the balance owed, request a meeting with a hospital case manager or someone from the accounts receivable department to express your concern. It is common for non-profit hospitals to waive a portion—or even the entirety—of the bill if you meet low-income qualifications. If you think you might qualify, do not hesitate to make this call, and consider *waiting* to pay your bill until your meeting. Because I believe in honoring one's debts, I am not suggesting you walk away from your bill, but you should consider negotiating with the hospital or medical provider if you feel you qualify for assistance or need assistance at your earliest opportunity. This will also help your credit report if you establish a workable and agreed-upon bill or payment method versus walking away from a debt.

One insurance carrier I (Rick) interviewed while researching this topic said that if the spouse or surviving family knows they will need financial assistance or the patient is under a Medicare Senior Advantage Plan, they should apply for "bill review and reduction" *before* death occurs to start the process. This may help lower co-pays or eliminate them completely. Knowing your patient's rights and the channels of support will help you through this challenging process, whether it is for billing or patient care.

Final Billing

Did you know it is common for a nursing home or assisted-living residence to not charge the resident, family, or estate the last month's fee when the resident reaches end-of-life? I (Rick) learned this when my dad died one day into his final month of residence. When I attempted to pay his last month's fee, they waived it and said, "Any time a resident reaches end-of-life, his or her last month's fee is waived as a way of saying thank you for allowing us to serve your family member." Does a hospital have a similar protocol? A major insurance carrier I interviewed said survivors typically pay for costs up to the point of death, and then there is no billing from that point forward.

In my research for this chapter and book, I found that people who classified themselves as "planners" resonated with the tasks at hand. Why? Because when you plan for almost any subject matter, you become informed, and as a result, make better decisions. This works well for individuals who naturally gravitate to research and planning, but what about others? I leave you with this encouragement if you are not a planner: Set goals for yourself, and with each week or month, accomplish those goals in small steps to minimize being overwhelmed when faced with end-of-life.

Action Steps

- Research whether or not you qualify for low-income subsidies, including discounted prescription drugs, and apply to those programs if you do.
- If you are planning to move to a new area or state, reviewing your medical coverage and needs to align with a hospital or medical facility in proximity could reduce the chance of needing care outside of your network.
- To maximize your coverage and options from your health plan, consider calling your agent for a complete review. Understanding your plan could save you money and lower stress, both emotionally and financially.

CHAPTER 11

Applying for Veteran Benefits

I have had the privilege to officiate services for veterans of the United States military at both Riverside National Cemetery and Sacramento Valley National Cemetery. My first veterans' service was for my brother, Rob, a veteran of the US Army. I was not the main officiant, but I played a role in the service.

My brother served in Vietnam in the northernmost base of South Vietnam—Pleiku, Camp Holloway—where he was a turbo jet mechanic working on helicopters. Less than a year after his return, he signed up for a mission that took him to Thailand after the war had officially ended. However, the reality was that the war continued, and he was part of it. His duties included working on helicopters and flying missions looking for POWs in areas of Laos and Cambodia. They never found them, but the effort alone exemplifies one of the core values of the military—no one left behind. My heart still grieves for these families who have yet to find complete closure.

After his three-year active-duty status and honorable discharge, he eventually went to work at a university in Southern California, trying to figure out the next step in life—like many vets. His job as sports turf manager was to maintain the sports fields and surrounding areas. He was good enough at his job to be recruited by a major league baseball player to work at his private winter camp for aspiring players, but he returned to the university after the entrepreneurial professional baseball player's adventure did not hit a home run—or even a double or single.

After years of civilian life, he came to discover that he had been exposed to Agent Orange while in Vietnam, and he had also been exposed to chemicals at his place of employment. His new illness kicked off a ten-year battle to survive. He was misdiagnosed for the first year with chronic symptoms believed to be respiratory-related. Once diagnosed properly with amyloidosis, he was then told treatment for amyloid patients was not available. But after extensive research, we learned there was a new treatment called "stem cell transplant" (he was number eighteen in the United States to have this procedure), but his medical insurance company would not cover this procedure because it was new, even though it was showing positive results. Our family collected donations and held numerous fundraisers, ranging from golf and bowling tournaments to a massive rummage sale at our church to pay the $72,000 price tag for his treatment.

Battles Take Place in Many Forms, Not Just on the Battlefield

After a successful but extremely difficult twenty-one days in Boston for his treatment, he returned to Southern California for recovery. As my brother battled his illness, he also took his battle to the California State Senate in Sacramento. The medical system did not allow for doctors to explain to their patients that even though a medical insurance company may not cover a treatment, there could be other treatments available. This was called the "gag rule" or "order," meaning there could be treatment options available, but because a medical insurance company did not cover those treatments, the attending doctor could not reveal other options. My brother's case successfully changed California state law. He was a fighter, but the chemical exposure he had experienced was significant, and his body yielded to the effects on March 21, 2006.

Pre-Need

Contact Your County Veteran Service Office

Did you know there is a County Veteran Service Office (CVSO) in almost every county in each state? My local office holds educational classes every week for veterans and their families to learn about the services available to those who qualify. Check with your local county office to see if they hold similar classes or one-on-one meetings with a counselor. As I researched for this chapter, I met with two veterans benefits counselors at two separate CVSOs and visited the Sacramento Valley National Cemetery.

One of the counselors I met told me a story about talking with a veteran who had been in contact with Agent Orange while in Vietnam. A friend had told him, "You won't qualify for any financial benefits, even though you have had a heart transplant, are on oxygen, and are disabled from Agent Orange." The veteran insisted the veterans benefits counselor was wasting his time because his friend had applied and had not received any benefits. The counselor repeatedly asked the veteran to make an appointment and come in to fill out the paperwork to get started. Unfortunately, the vet wasn't physically able due to his disability, so the counselor went to his house to serve him. A few months later, the counselor received a phone call from the veteran, announcing he had just received a check for over $500,000 due to his Agent Orange encounter and subsequent disability. Moral of the story: Let the CVSO counselor tell you what you will and will not qualify for, not a friend! And, let your local CVSO counselor help you file all the paperwork to get you started in the system. They can do it right, which will save you time and frustration and potentially allow you to receive compensation.

As I spoke with each veterans benefits counselor, I quickly realized these people are single-focused in their mission to serve you, the veterans, and your families. Their role in this giant machine called Veterans Administration (VA) is to get the veterans and their families served to the best of their ability. They do not make the rules, but they know how to work within the rules, and they have answers—or can get them. They have passion because they are also veterans, or they work in that office because of their love for veterans.

Register as a Veteran

While there are many benefits available to veterans during their lifetime, in this chapter, I'll focus on benefits related to end-of-life. If you have not already registered for any type of benefit (you are not in the system), visit your local (CVSO) and take these items with you to get started:

- Your DD214 (discharge) paperwork.
- Your marriage and, if applicable, divorce paperwork.
- Marital history on both sides of your family.
- Banking information for direct deposit.

Veterans can also "sponsor" applications for their spouse or dependent children.

Apply for Burial in a VA Cemetery

The following information has been adapted from the VA website https://www.va.gov/burials-memorials/eligibility/[1] and https://www.va.gov/burials-memorials/pre-need-eligibility/.[2]

In addition to applying for benefits, veterans may apply in advance for burial in a VA national cemetery. Veterans, service members, spouses, and dependents may qualify for burial in a VA national cemetery and other benefits if they meet one of the requirements listed below.

The person qualifying for burial benefits is:

- A veteran who didn't receive a dishonorable discharge.
- A service member who died while on active duty, active duty for training, or inactive duty for training.
- The spouse or minor child of a veteran.
- In some cases, the unmarried adult dependent child of a veteran.

To apply, you'll need your (or your sponsor's):

- Social Security number.
- Date and place of birth.
- Military status and service history (like service dates, discharge character, and rank).
- Discharge papers (DD214 or other separation documents).

More than four million people are buried in VA cemeteries. Burial locations are assigned based on availability at the time of need. Although veterans cannot reserve a gravesite, they can indicate a cemetery preference. Doing so allows VA officials to predict need at cemeteries and may assist with decision-making for those choosing a burial site after the veteran's death. The pre-determination process qualifies veterans for burial in 135 cemeteries and 33 soldiers' lots operated by the VA nationwide. You can apply online or by mail using VA form 40-10007. For a list of VA National Cemetery Locations, visit http://www.va.gov/directory/guide/division_flsh.asp?dnum=4.

Note that this process does not include Arlington National Cemetery (ANC), which is operated by the US Army and uses a different application system. The process to schedule a burial at ANC can be complex. Scheduling military funeral services at ANC is primarily influenced by three factors: the type of remains, military resources available, and preferences of the individual family. Services for active-duty service members who die of hostile wounds are scheduled first. Services for active-duty service members, regardless of the manner of death, are handled next. Veterans and family members with casketed remains are subsequently scheduled, followed by services with cremated remains. ANC schedules casketed burials within three weeks of receiving the request for burial. The service takes place when the military funeral honors for which the veteran is eligible are available. For cremated remains, wait times are as long as nine to eleven months for a service requiring military funeral honors with a funeral escort, and up to seven to eight months for a military funeral honors service without funeral escort or a dependent honors service.

For more information on Arlington National Cemetery, go to https://www.arlingtoncemetery.mil/Funerals/About-Funerals.[3]

For information about the Navy's burial at sea program, visit https://www.mynavyhr.navy.mil/Support-Services/Casualty/Mortuary-Services/Burial-at-Sea/.[4]

To learn how to schedule a burial for a veteran or family member, go to https://www.va.gov/burials-memorials/schedule-a-burial/.[5]

At-Need

The information in this section has been adapted from the Veterans Administration website, www.va.gov/burials-memorials/veterans-burial-allowance/.[6] As a disclaimer, due to potential changes by the VA, you should contact your CVSO or the VA website to verify the information for accuracy. The national number for the Veterans Administration is 1-800-827-1000. For a full list of contact numbers by department, visit https://www.va.gov/resources/helpful-va-phone-numbers/.

Burial Benefits

The VA offers a burial allowance to cover the costs of a funeral, burial in a national cemetery, the plot (gravesite) or interment, and transporting the remains. The veteran's family will need to cover the cost of funeral director services like cremation.

If you are a surviving spouse or beneficiary of a veteran, contact your county office upon the veteran's death—even if the veteran never filed a claim while he or she was alive. The VA will automatically process burial benefits for "known" veterans, but they are incapable of serving veterans who are not registered in the system.

You can find more details about burial benefits at the U.S. Department of Veterans Affairs website http://www.cem.va.gov/burial_benefits.[7] Visit www.vets.gov for extensive information on costs and what is covered.

Who Can File a Claim

If you are applying for a burial allowance, one of these relationships or professional roles must describe your connection to the veteran. You're:

- The veteran's surviving spouse (the VA recognizes same-sex marriages).
- The surviving partner from a legal union (a relationship made formal in a document issued by the state recognizing the union).
- A surviving child of the veteran.
- A parent of the veteran.
- The executor or administrator of the veteran's estate (someone who officially represents the veteran).

You don't need to file a claim as a surviving spouse as long as you're listed as the veteran's spouse on the veteran's profile. When the VA receives notice of the veteran's death, they automatically pay a set amount to those eligible surviving spouses.

If you're applying on behalf of someone else, you'll need supporting documents showing you have the authority to apply for that person by filling out one of these forms: Appointment of Veterans Service Organization as Claimant's Representative (VA Form 21–22) or Appointment of Individual as Claimant's Representative (VA Form 21–22a).

To qualify for a burial allowance, the veteran must not have received a dishonorable discharge, and one of these circumstances must be true. The veteran died:

- As a result of a service-connected disability.
- While getting VA care, either at a VA facility or at a facility contracted by VA.
- While traveling with proper authorization, and at VA expense, either to or from a facility for an examination or to receive treatment or care.
- With an original or reopened claim for VA compensation or pension pending at the time of death, if he or she would've been entitled to benefits before the time of death.
- While receiving VA pension or compensation.

- While eligible for VA pension or compensation at time of death, but instead received full military retirement or disability pay.

The VA doesn't provide burial allowances if the individual died:
- On active duty.
- While serving as a member of Congress.
- While serving a federal prison sentence.

When to File a Claim

You must file a claim for a non-service-connected burial allowance within two years after the veteran's burial or cremation. If a veteran's discharge was changed after death from dishonorable to another status, you must file for an allowance claim within two years after the discharge update. There's no time limit to file for a service-connected burial allowance.

How to Apply

You can apply online for a burial allowance at https://www. va.gov/burials-and-memorials/application/530/introduction. You'll need copies of the following documents:
- The veteran's military discharge papers (DD214 or other separation documents).
- The veteran's death certificate.
- Any documents or receipts you have for the cost of transporting the veteran's remains.
- A statement of account (preferably with the letterhead of the funeral director or cemetery owner) that has the veteran's name, the type of service or item purchased, any credits, and the unpaid balance.

Allowance Amounts

Burial allowance amounts vary based on factors, such as whether the death was service-connected or non-service-connected.

For the most up-to-date information, visit https://www.va.gov/burials-memorials/veterans-burial-allowance/.[8] Keep in mind that it is common for a funeral home to bill survivors directly while waiting for payment from the VA. Why? Because payment from the VA to funeral homes is traditionally slow. You may need to pay the funeral home directly while waiting for the VA to reimburse your out-of-pocket cost.

Military Funeral Honors

Most veteran burials begin with a committal service. When you arrive at the cemetery, a cemetery representative will meet you and give you the deceased's burial documents. They'll lead you and others who are gathered to honor the deceased to a committal shelter. The committal service takes place at this location, not at the gravesite, and lasts for about thirty minutes. The burial happens after the committal service. You may request to have military funeral honors performed at the committal shelter. These may include a rifle detail, playing "Taps," and presentation of a burial flag by uniformed service members. Arrange for military funeral honors through your funeral director or get help from a CVSO or from VA national cemetery staff. Note that viewing facilities are not available at national cemeteries, so if a family would like a staged viewing of their loved one, then those arrangements must be made with a funeral home before the day of the service at the national cemetery.

Headstones and Markers

A veteran who didn't receive a dishonorable discharge or a service member who died while on active duty may be eligible for a headstone or marker if he or she meets the requirements listed below specific to when he or she served.

For enlisted personnel who served before September 7, 1980, and officers who served before October 16, 1981, at least one of these must be true. The veteran or service member:

- Died on or after November 1, 1990, and his or her grave is currently marked with a privately purchased headstone.
- Was buried in an unmarked grave, anywhere in the world.

Note: If the veteran or service member served before World War I, the VA requires detailed documents like muster rolls, extracts from state files, or the military or state organization where he or she served.

For enlisted personnel who served after September 7, 1980, and officers who served after October 16, 1981, at least one of these must be true. The veteran or service member:

- Died on or after November 1, 1990, and his or her grave is currently marked with a privately purchased headstone.
- Was buried in an unmarked grave, anywhere in the world.

And at least one of these must also be true. The veteran or service member:

- Served for a minimum of twenty-four months of continuous active duty.
- Died while serving on active duty.

Note: Hmong individuals who were living in the US when they died are eligible if they were naturalized under the Hmong Veterans Naturalization Act of 2000 and died on or after March 23, 2018.

To learn more about available "Emblems of Belief" for placement on government headstones and markers, go to https://www.cem.va.gov/cem/hmm/emblems.asp.[9]

Burial Flags

Generally, the burial flag is given to the next-of-kin as a keepsake after its use during the funeral service. When there is no next-of-kin, the VA will furnish the flag to a friend who makes a request for it. For those VA national cemeteries with an Avenue of Flags, families of veterans buried in these national cemeteries may donate the burial flags of their loved ones to be flown on

patriotic holidays. Learn more at https://www.cem.va.gov/cem/
burial_benefits/burial_flags.asp.[10]

A Note from Rick
The title of United States veteran is not one that
can be given; it can only be earned. For all the
active servicemen and women, your service today
keeps us free as a nation. I pray this never changes.
Thank you. For all the brave men and women who
have earned the title of veteran, we honor and
appreciate you—in life and death.

Action Steps

- Make an appointment with a CVSO counselor and register as a veteran.
- Apply in advance for burial in a VA cemetery if that is your wish. Determine what you would like written on your headstone or marker and tell your family about any military funeral honors you wish to have.
- If you are a survivor who is at-need, apply for a burial allowance and any survivor benefits you may be eligible for.

CHAPTER 12

Accessing Social Security Benefits

There is a saying I learned years ago in the business world, and I learned it the hard way: "Expect what you don't inspect." Simply said, if you fail to investigate, you should not be surprised when the unexpected becomes reality. It did for me when I visited the Social Security Administration (SSA) for a benefit for which I thought I was eligible.

My personal experience with the SSA through the death of my wife, mom, and dad proved to be an informative experience—but it was a learning curve. After the death of my wife, Susie, I did not fully grasp the information I received over the phone from an SSA representative. At my scheduled appointment with a representative, I came armed with questions to gain insight into my wife's accumulated investment into the system over her working career. I learned I was eligible to receive her SSA retirement income, which was greater than my personal anticipated SSA retirement income, but there were stipulations. Here is where the breakdown occurred. Either the complicated criteria were not made clear during our appointment or I failed to absorb and process the quantity of information presented while grieving. As a result, I would not benefit from her decades of hard work and paying into Social Security, leaving her investment absorbed into the system. Am I blaming anyone at SSA? No, just myself for not investigating further to fully understand the criteria. I relied on my incomplete homework and the SSA representative. That was my mistake, and I own it.

I hope my mistakes help you make wise choices to maximize your benefits.

When my dad died on May 1, 2017, I was in a much better place emotionally to deal with his end-of-life business affairs. Having gone through the death of my brother, wife, mom, and now my dad, I researched online and read about retiring my dad's Social Security number and receiving his last monthly retirement check and one-time death benefit. Armed with all the necessary paperwork, I made an appointment with an SSA representative, and within fifteen to twenty minutes, the business was finished. I made sure to leave his checking account open until the final check was deposited (I highly encourage you to contact the SSA about the decedent's last month's check. Why? Because the SSA will withdraw the last check deposited because each check is for the previous month's earned distribution). Separate of the SSA information above, failure to have the same account open to receive final installments from any institution requires requesting the check payable to a different financial institution with a new account holder. This makes it exceedingly difficult—if not impossible—to do transactions concluding the decedent's business affairs.

With a system as complicated as Social Security Administration, planning for end-of-life and equipping yourself ahead of time becomes even more important. Whether you are planning pre-need or at-need, this chapter will help you learn about the benefits offered through the SSA.

How Social Security Works

The Social Security Administration is a federal government agency that offers retirement, disability, Medicare, and supplemental security income (SSI) benefits. Some of these benefits are transferrable to survivors after a person dies. Spouses, parents, and dependents can qualify for survivor benefits. The focus of this chapter will be on benefits as they relate to survivors after end-of-life.

Most of the information in this chapter has been sourced from the Social Security Administration (SSA) website found at www.

ssa.gov. It is your responsibility as the reader to do your own research. This is how you learn and take ownership of the process. Once you review the SSA website, you will see the complexity created by the criteria for eligibility. But do not give up if you have a need because your due diligence can be rewarded.

Retirement Benefits

The following information has been adapted from the SSA website https://www.ssa.gov/benefits/retirement/learn.html#h1.[1]

Social Security replaces a percentage of a worker's pre-retirement income based on his or her lifetime earnings. The portion of your pre-retirement wages that Social Security replaces is based on your highest thirty-five years of earnings and varies depending on how much you earn and when you choose to start benefits.

The Social Security system works like this: when you work, you pay taxes into Social Security. The SSA uses the tax money to pay benefits to:
- People who have already retired.
- People who are disabled.
- Survivors of workers who have died.
- Dependents of beneficiaries.

The money you pay in taxes isn't held in a personal account for you to use when you get benefits. The SSA uses your taxes to pay people who are getting benefits right now. Any unused money goes to a Social Security trust fund that pays monthly benefits to you and your family when you start receiving retirement benefits.

Eligibility and Credits

The following information has been adapted from the SSA website https://www.ssa.gov/planners/credits.html.[2]

You qualify for Social Security benefits by earning Social Security credits when you work and pay Social Security taxes. You must earn at least forty Social Security credits to qualify for Social Security benefits. The number of credits does not affect the amount of benefits you receive. It only determines if you are eligible or not.

The SSA bases Social Security credits on the amount of your earnings. They use your earnings and work history to determine your eligibility for retirement, disability benefits, or your family's eligibility for survivor's benefits when you die. In 2021, you receive one credit for each $1,470 of earnings, up to a maximum of four credits per year. Each year the amount of earnings needed for credits goes up slightly as average earnings levels increase. The credits you earn remain on your Social Security record even if you change jobs or have no earnings for a while.

Special rules for earning Social Security coverage apply to certain types of work. If you are self-employed, you earn Social Security credits the same way employees do. Special rules apply if you have net annual earnings of less than $400. If you are in the military, you earn Social Security credits the same way civilian employees do. You may also get additional earnings credits under certain conditions.

The SSA also has special rules about how you earn credits for other kinds of work. Some of these jobs are: domestic work, farm work, or work for a church or church-controlled organization that does not pay Social Security taxes.

History of the Lump-Sum Death Benefit

The following information has been adapted from https:// www.fool.com/retirement/2018/05/23/the-strangest-social-security-benefit-you-can-get.aspx.[3]

In the original 1935 legislation that created Social Security, there were no ongoing survivor benefits for family members after a worker passed away. Therefore, the lump-sum death benefit was added, equal to 3.5 percent of the deceased worker's covered earnings. That worked out to a maximum amount of $315, although the average in the late 1930s was about $97.

When recurring survivor benefits got added to the program in 1940, the original variable lump-sum death benefit was replaced with a one-time payment equal to six times the worker's primary insurance amount. The intent was that the payment would help surviving family members who weren't eligible for the new survivor benefits and would provide burial expenses for non-family members if there wasn't anyone in the family to claim the lump sum. Payments ranged from $64 to $274, with the average being about $146.

It wasn't until 1954 that the $255 cap on the lump-sum death benefit was established. The reason had to do with the rise in monthly benefit payments, which would have greatly increased the death benefit without the imposition of a separate limit. At the time, most calculated death benefit amounts were less than $255, so the lower amount was paid. Even today, current law states that the benefit can be lower than $255 if that number is greater than three times the primary insurance amount for the deceased worker.

This one-time payment of $255 is paid in addition to any monthly cash benefits due. The lump-sum death payment is paid in the following "priority," according to the SSA website:

- A surviving spouse who lived in the same household as the deceased person at the time of death.
- A surviving spouse eligible for or entitled to benefits for the month of death.
- A child or children eligible for or entitled to benefits for the month of death.

SSDI and SSI

The loss of a family member goes beyond the emotional grieving that takes place; it could also mean the loss of income or benefits. For some individuals, applying for SSA benefits beyond the SSA retirement plan that many enjoy can include Social Security Disability Insurance (SSDI) or Supplemental Security Income (SSI). It is not uncommon for your initial application for either SSDI or SSI to be denied. In fact, two-thirds are denied automatically. Answering the question "why" would require another entire chapter, so I will move on to explaining both benefits.

What's the Difference?

SSDI is available to workers who qualify through accumulating the necessary number of work credits, meaning, they have paid into the Social Security trust fund called FICA Social Security Tax. Conversely, SSI is a program offering disability benefits to low-income qualified individuals who do not meet the criteria earning the necessary work credits for SSDI or do not have an income history. Even though there is a commonality—both coming from the Social Security Administration—they are vastly different through funding and criteria for qualification. Funding for SSDI is paid through payroll taxes (FICA Social Security Tax) while SSI is funded through "general taxes," which do not come from the Social Security trust fund. A simpler view of these two benefits is: SSDI is an earned benefit, and SSI is based on financial needs, with funding coming from two different sources.

Qualification Criteria

SSDI disability qualifications take into consideration age, type of disability, and work credits accumulated. Most recipients are deemed eligible if they have a significant, long-term, or total disability claim. The waiting period before receiving the first check for those who qualify is five months.

SSI is awarded to those who qualify based on financial need (this program is also referred to as a "need-based" program), whether adult or child, who are disabled or meet the qualifications for low income. The SSA also requires a recipient to be a US citizen who meets the criteria set by the SSA. SSI may also differ from state to state, so check with your local SSA office or website for clarification.

The following table, taken from the SSA website at https://www.ssa.gov/redbook/eng/overview-disability.htm,[4] compares the SSDI and SSI disability programs.

	SSDI	SSI
Source of Payments	Disability trust fund	General tax revenues
Minimum Initial Qualification Requirements	It must meet Social Security's disability criteria; must be "insured" due to contributions made to FICA based on your own earnings, or those of your spouse or your parents.	It must meet Social Security's disability criteria; must have limited income and resources.
Health Insurance Coverage Provided	Medicare; consists of hospital insurance (Part A), supplementary medical insurance (Part B), and Medicare Advantage (Part C). Voluntary prescription drug benefits (Part D) are also included. Title XVIII of the Social Security Act authorizes Medicare.	Medicaid; a jointly-funded, Federal-State health insurance program for persons with limited income and resources. It covers certain children and some or all of the aged, blind, and disabled in a state who are eligible to receive federally-assisted income maintenance payments. Title XIX of the Social Security Act authorizes Medicaid. The law gives the states options regarding eligibility under Medicaid.

	SSDI	SSI
How Do We Figure Your Monthly Payment Amount?	We base your SSDI monthly payment amount on the worker's lifetime average earnings covered by Social Security. We may reduce the amount if you receive Workers' Compensation payments (including Black Lung payments) or public disability benefits, for example, certain state and civil service disability benefits. Other income or resources do not affect your payment amount. We usually adjust the monthly payment amount each year to account for cost-of-living changes. We can also pay SSDI monthly benefits to dependents on your record, such as minor children.	To figure your payment amount, we start with the Federal Benefit Rate (FBR). In 2019, the FBR is $771 for a qualified person and $1,157 for a qualified couple. We subtract your countable income from the FBR and then add your state supplement, if any. We do not count all of the income that you have. The income amount left after we make all the allowable deductions is "countable income." The sections on SSI employment supports explain some of the ways that we can exclude income. We usually adjust the FBR each year to account for cost-of-living changes.

	SSDI	SSI
Is a State Supplemental Payment Provided?	There is no state supplemental payment with the SSDI program.	Many states pay some persons who receive SSI an additional amount called a "state supplement." The amounts and qualifications for these state supplements vary from state to state.

Applying for Benefits

This simple statement from the SSA, "You must apply in order to receive benefits," is your first indicator that *you* must take the first step in the process. You may apply at any Social Security office by telephone at 1-800-772-1213 or online at www.ssa.gov. When you contact the SSA, they may require you to have the following documentation when applying for benefits:

- Your Social Security number and the number of the deceased.
- Birth certificate of the deceased.
- Marriage certificate.
- Divorce certificate, if applicable.
- Certificate of death.

I recommend going directly to the source for accurate information and education. The sites below will assist you in generating questions, finding answers and current information on benefits, and updating your personal information.

- Benefit Finder
  A questionnaire designed to assist you in finding what benefits you qualify for.
  https://www.benefits.gov/

- Benefit Eligibility Screening Tool
  Find out what benefits you may be eligible for through Social Security. https://ssabest.benefits.gov/

- Social Security Administration
  Use this website to create your own account and apply for a Social Security number and benefits. It also has several tools like a retirement estimator, FAQs, and blog. https://www.ssa.gov/

- The Financial Literacy and Education Commission
  This website offers mentoring on finances for a variety of scenarios. In addition, it counsels people who are "Rebuilding Your Finances After A Disaster." https://www.mymoney.gov/About-Us

When you make your appointment to meet with a representative, be prepared to ask questions about your life situation, such as:

- My spouse died—can I receive his or her monthly SSA retirement check, and what are the stipulations? Does the surviving spouse have to wait until he or she is of retirement age, or does the surviving spouse benefit from having a spouse who was older and start the benefit at the deceased's qualifying age?
- If my spouse dies, what medical benefits can I receive, either for me or a qualified family member, and who are the qualified family members?
- What financial assistance will my minor child receive in relation to the deceased? As a minor under age eighteen, what education benefits are available? If over eighteen years old, what education benefits are available, and what are the stipulations?
- What benefits are available for disabled survivors?
- How long does it take after applying for the lump-sum death payment to arrive?
- Can I receive benefits as a divorced spouse of the deceased? What if I'm widowed and planning to remarry?

Keep in mind that you will probably have more questions resulting from your appointment than when you walked in! The list of questions you develop should come from educating yourself through personal research and conversations with others who have gone through the death of a loved one. When you consider that people hire attorneys to assist them with benefits they feel are earned or they are entitled to, it says something about the complexity of the system, so be prepared by educating yourself before you visit your local SSA office. Keep in mind—*the SSA office will not take the role of asking you questions to maximize your potential benefits.* I cannot stress this enough because of my experience and that of others I've spoken with. SSA employees are good people but are working within a system that can be cumbersome. They can be helpful, but maximizing your benefits does not appear to be part of their job—only processing your application. You may find it helpful to obtain outside counsel to navigate through the regulations.

Action Steps

- Check for the number of "credits" you have accumulated so you know exactly what is required for you to reach the forty-credit minimum to qualify for your full benefit(s).
- Research Social Security benefits as they relate to your situation and develop a list of questions.
- Whether you are planning pre-need or at-need, make an appointment with your local SSA representative and take a trusted friend who can take notes as you ask questions. Ask the representative to show you where on the SSA website you can find the information shared for future reference.
- If your spouse (or former spouse) has died and you are considering remarrying, ask your SSA representative how this affects the benefits you receive from your deceased spouse. This is critical for future planning.

CHAPTER 13

Grieving Your Loss

I had felt pain before, but not like this.

When my wife Susie died, she had been living with and fighting cancer for over fifteen years. She'd had multiple hospital visits and warnings that she was getting close or wouldn't be coming home from the hospital, only to rally again. So, you would think that on April 24, 2007, I would have been prepared to say, "I'll see you again one day," then hear her last breath. Not so!

Her death came just thirteen months after the passing of my brother, who died from complications due to Agent Orange exposure in Vietnam while serving in the US Army. Six months after Susie, my mom passed unexpectedly while in rehab from back surgery. Through human error, she was given food to take with a pill when her medical chart clearly said, "No Food." A food particle found its way into her lung, causing massive infection, and she died within two days after ingestion.

During this difficult time, the words of Dr. Paul David Tripp, a pastor, speaker, and author, captured how I felt. In his video presentation for the GriefShare recovery group, he said: "If I'm in my basement on a bright sunny day, and the shades in the basement are pulled, and so it's pitch dark down there—the sun hasn't ceased to shine at all. There is something 'at the moment' that has clouded my ability to see the sun. That's what grief does."[1] I (Rick) felt like I was living in that proverbial basement with the window treatments closed, blocking out the sunlight, yet knowing there was light on the other side, begging to shine in. How was I going to work through the grief when I could not see the sunlight?

The elders at our church expressed their deep love and concern for me with an incredible gift by sending me to a ministry called Blessing Ranch in Colorado (now in Florida), founded by Dr. John Walker—a licensed psychologist and ordained pastor. His ministry is to pastors and missionaries, and he works alongside his daughter, Dr. Charity Byers, also a licensed psychologist. After a week with Dr. John, which included a session every morning for four hours, then homework in the afternoon and an evening meal with his family, I left for home with hope. The sun started to penetrate the window of my heart.

Over the course of the next several weeks, I also met with one of our church members who is a licensed psychologist to talk about my emotional health and my next steps. He made a comment to me about still wearing my wedding ring: "One day you will take it off, and when you do, that's another big step forward." I couldn't imagine taking it off, but eight months later, I did, and he noticed that Sunday at church. With a smile that indicated his approval, he said, "Good for you."

> Billy Graham, often referred to as America's pastor, wrote in his book *Death and the Life After*, "Time doesn't heal . . . It's what you do with the time that heals."[3]

Grief is unique in a person's life relating to how you process and live out Reverend Graham's charge. I caution you not to compare your grief journey to mine. I had thirty to forty hours of intense therapy in Colorado, numerous hours with my friend, the psychologist, and counseling from the senior pastor at my church. Is this also your answer to find healing as you grieve? Possibly, but you need to find what works for you, so keep talking with professionals and keep submitting yourself to the grief journey process, which, although painful, is normal and healthy. I encourage you to read grief books and website articles to understand the components and potential paths to health. And keep sharing with friends how you are feeling today. Tomorrow will come, so focus on today!

My professional co-author for this chapter is Kathryn Denham, a licensed clinical social worker (LCSW). As a LCSW, she provides individual, group, and family therapy to assess, diagnose, treat, and prevent mental illness and emotional and behavioral disturbances. She has over thirty-two years of experience treating a wide variety of issues, including grief. I met her when I was building a network of therapists for our GriefShare group at church to refer group members for support. I immediately liked her, both because of her compassion for people and in-depth knowledge of grief counseling. To offer just a glimpse of Kathryn's willingness to help, we invited her to share at one of our GriefShare meetings, and she did this without charge—it was a gift for us!

Preparing for Loss

(Kathryn) Grieving is one of the most challenging experiences in life—and yet, it is also inevitable. In his book *The 5 Things We Cannot Change*, David Richo, PhD, a psychotherapist, addresses grief as a "given" in life. "There are five unavoidable givens, five immutable facts that come to visit all of us many times over: 1. Everything changes and ends. 2. Things do not always go according to plan. 3. Life is not always fair. 4. Pain is part of life. 5. People are not loving and loyal all the time . . . These are the core challenges that we all face. But too often we live in denial of these facts."[2]

The more we accept these givens of life, the less we will suffer from unmet expectations. The true reality is that we all experience loss, and we need to take the time to grieve the loss in our lives. Grieving is an integral part of life. It is not "if" we will experience hard times; it is "when."

It's been said that we grieve to the degree that we have loved the person we lost. The more you were attached to one another, the more severe the grief experience will be. If we had not loved the person so deeply, then we would not be feeling such great sorrow and emotional pain. As a result, you will be on a journey of healing and restoration for a long period of time—and that is normal.

It is important to prepare as much as possible for the loss of our loved ones. If we have our affairs in order, then when a loved one passes away, we will have a greater opportunity to focus on who he or she was as a valued family member or friend in our lives. We can take the time to sit and be still with our feelings. But, if we have not taken the time to get organized prior to his or her passing, then we will be experiencing tremendous chaos and confusion in handling the necessary tasks at hand. Death doesn't always adhere to our timing; therefore, meeting with family members when "all is well" to express your desires will promote a healthier grieving process for the survivors when the time comes.

> *A Note from Rick*
> *I agree wholeheartedly with Kathryn on preparation. If you have read the previous chapters, then you know Susie and I had prepared for her end-of-life for years. I also recognized that my grief started years prior to her death, anticipating the day when she would no longer be with us. Did knowing her cancer would shorten her life help or hurt with my grief? I cannot honestly say if the foreknowledge shortened or lengthened my grief, but this I do know: My grief was not a surprise, but the depth and length of my grief was more intense than anticipated. In retrospect, I now understand and appreciate our perseverance in planning our affairs. It offered me a greater chance to grieve in a healthy way rather than through the chaos of emotions and business affairs that begin immediately upon death.*
>
> *What I did not do as part of my planning for her death was to seek counseling prior to that event. As your loved one is dying, it's common to feel that the pain in you is greater than in the one dying!*

Advance counseling about what to expect with the death of a loved one can be extremely beneficial in steering you through the process of grieving. It helps reduce the unknown, allowing you to accept the intense feelings and go with the process versus fighting the process. Even if you choose not to begin counseling prior to death, researching and finding a counselor in advance can be helpful. Then, if you do seek counseling after the death of your loved one, you have already found a professional who takes your insurance and is aware of your current life circumstances.

Understanding Grief

So, what is grief? Simply stated, it is the response to a loss of a loved one who is dear to us, or to a change of circumstances of any kind, such as divorce, loss of a job, loss of pets, loss of friendships, aspirations and expectations not met, and so much more. Loss is an integral part of life. It also brings on a change of circumstance when our loved one or the object of our loss is no longer present. Significant grief responses that go unresolved can lead to mental, physical, and sociological problems, potentially contributing to family dysfunction across generations; therefore, seek help during the grief process to assist you on your journey to a healthy recovery.

The five commonly recognized stages of grief are:
1. Shock and denial.
2. Anger.
3. Bargaining.
4. Depression.
5. Acceptance.

A Note from Rick
Some therapists will include guilt in this list. The guilt stage of grief refers to feelings of regret

about difficult aspects of the relationship with the deceased. When death occurs suddenly, you may lose the opportunity to resolve past pains and old hurts, which can cause guilt and suffering to linger. Settling issues prior to death can aid in "letting go" as you journey through the grief process. If your loved one has died prior to working through relational challenges, those hurts and pains may still exist, but it does not mean they must remain. Meeting with a knowledgeable therapist to work through these issues can still usher in emotional freedom from the past—to some degree, or maybe complete freedom. I encourage you to take this step because choosing to live with these negative thoughts and experiences can, and probably will, affect your perspective on life. Make the choice today. Contact someone for help.

The path is not always linear, but rather a moving forward and reversing and repeating of the process. It takes time and consistent effort to feel our feelings move through the stages of grieving, and we cannot do it alone. We need a safe place with loved ones, family, and friends to process our feelings.

To better understand the work involved in the process of grieving in a simplistic manner—although there is nothing simple about the actual process—I use the acronym TEAR:

T = To accept the reality of the loss
E = Experience the pain and agony of the loss
A = Adjust to the new lifestyle without their loved one
R = Reinvest in the new reality

Each step in this process is chronological, but like the stages of grief, the process is one that involves taking small steps forward with occasional steps backward. Repeating these steps does not mean you are regressing. Over time, these steps backward are measurably less and become increasingly bearable, allowing the person to continue his or her grief journey in a healthy way.

Grief Responses

Each of us engages in a unique process of grieving and healing. We will experience a variety of feelings and sensations throughout the healing journey, and these may come and go intermittently. The symptoms of grief can be displayed in many ways—physical, emotional, and psychological.

Physical Responses

- Feeling tightness in the throat or heaviness in the chest.
- Having an empty feeling in the stomach and loss of appetite, turning to food as a comfort, and snacking throughout the day.
- Having difficulty sleeping and feeling exhausted throughout the day.

Grieving can have a profound impact on your physical health. It is common to give in and eat junk food for comfort or convenience or eat extraordinarily little and infrequently, so be intentional about staying healthy and get help if needed. Drink plenty of fluids, like water or juice, but limit alcohol consumption to avoid problems in the future and maintain clarity. Exercise regularly if possible, and if needed, meet with your doctor to discuss a healthy exercise routine. If you have pre-existing health conditions, make sure you are keeping up with your medication or treatments.

Emotional Responses

- Defensiveness. This emotion fights emerging feelings.
- Depression. Depression increases when we isolate, which is normal, but the healthy approach is to reach out to others to help prevent self-isolation.
- Negative self-talk. Focus on engaging and being grateful for the past to avoid the spiral of depression and negative energy.
- Crying. Crying is a gift. Tears honor your loss and represent our humanity. They also help relieve pent-up

emotional pressure in a healthy way. It is okay to cry until the need to cry has subsided.

- Vulnerability. All death leaves a person lonely and vulnerable—especially men, surprisingly. Men are prone to look for a relationship before the grieving is over.
- Anger. Helplessness turning to anger and frustration or lashing out is known as "kick the dog" syndrome.
- Regret. Having thoughts of "would have, could have, should have" can cause you to blame yourself for the loss of your loved one.
- Mood Swings. Grief can cause your mood to change over the slightest things.

Psychological Responses

- Feeling restless and looking for activities to engage in but finding it difficult to concentrate.
- Turning to addictive substances such as alcohol, drugs, food, technology, busyness, and so on.
- Feeling as though the loss is not real.
- Longing for and fantasizing about what might have been, often constructing a better outcome.
- Feeling as though you need to take care of other people who seem uncomfortable around you by politely not talking about difficult feelings and memories.
- Needing to tell and retell stories of the experience, memories, or insights.
- Experiencing an intense preoccupation with details of remembered events.
- Wandering aimlessly and often forgetting things.
- Not finishing things you've started.

Finding Support

For survivors, end-of-life can be traumatic. Grieving and bereavement often leave a person searching for answers. Rather than turning to substance abuse, a reclusive lifestyle, or an obsessive addiction as a means of relief, seek a counselor who specializes in end-of-life, a house of worship to answer questions you have, or trusted friends who know you well enough to identify areas of your life that have become unhealthy. Taking these positive steps will assist you in avoiding unhealthy patterns of life that can become destructive. Nobody is immune to pain; therefore, nobody is immune to making bad decisions. Get help!

Despite your negative feelings about yourself during this time, you are loveable even when you feel like a confused mess. Feeling down, alone, sad, cranky, moody, tired, hopeless, angry, and confused does not mean you are a failure. It means you are feeling what you should be feeling after a loss, and those closest to you will recognize your pain but still appreciate and love you as a person, and probably even more because of their deep love for you.

The Discomfort of Grief

Due to the lack of cultural teaching and expressions of grief, it is common for people to feel uncomfortable around those who are grieving. Sometimes people avoid being around a grieving person to minimize their own uncomfortable feelings about loss. They often do not have any idea what to say or are afraid their response(s) may trigger negative feelings and emotions. As a result, they maintain their distance. If people are uncomfortable with your grief, it is their problem and not yours. It is not helpful to blame someone who will not, cannot, or does not know how to comfort you.

Instead, find someone who will take this journey with you—who won't try to fix you because that is not his or her role.

A Note from Rick
My experience with loss and grief involves both types of responses from friends and loved ones. Those I thought might be the most comforting were not due to the uncomfortable nature of the circumstance, while others I thought would be less compassionate were just the opposite. Both

groups of people were wonderful but responded based on their personalities, cultural and professional training (or lack thereof), compassion, and level of willingness to be uncomfortable. Those who work through their discomfort tend to focus on the person grieving instead of themselves. Your experience may lead to a greater appreciation for those willing to step in and help while you embrace this journey.

Not long after Susie died, I had lunch with a friend from church—a hand surgeon who worked at a local hospital. He was one of those people I didn't expect to be comforting, but he asked me questions about where I was in the grief process. Answering, I became very emotional and began to cry, which should not be a surprise to anyone on this journey. But what did surprise me was when he took my hand and listened intently. Then as I finished my sharing, I withdrew my hand. To this day—and I still laugh about it—I wonder if he was really looking at my wrist, which I'd permanently damaged in an accident. I appreciated his attention and expression of love, but I'm still dealing with the wrist pain!

The Ministry of Presence

I (Rick) also learned during my grief journey(s) the importance of having someone to talk with, such as a friend who will just listen and not try to analyze or fix me. If you are on this journey of recovery, find one or two people and establish a relationship with boundaries for success. Simply explain that their role on this journey is to "listen, listen some more, and keep listening" until you are tired of talking. I call this the "ministry of presence" and would describe it this way:

*The ministry of presence may be the most difficult
ministry of all. It requires you to say nothing—your
thoughts remain thoughts, your motivation to speak
is suppressed, and your need to fix a person is recognized for what it is: your yearning to see the
person whole again. When the ministry of presence
is exercised, a heart of compassion becomes your
gift as you sit silently listening, letting the silence
speak for itself. Your gift of presence becomes the
strength he or she needs, and your ear the counselor that has been recommended.*

This may sound strange, opposing human nature and what you
have been taught in the past, but the safe environment of silence
has helped me and many others. Having this safe environment
offers you a chance to express yourself (the survivor) rather than
holding in your emotions. Having this freedom is a natural way
of releasing, providing it is to the right person(s). Include in your
boundaries that what is discussed stays between you and them, not
to be shared unless you give permission or are expressing emotions or intent that could bring harm to you or others. Bringing
someone with a history of breaking confidentiality into your inner
circle will only create more negative emotions and pain, so choose
wisely and set clear boundaries. Isn't it true that when given a task,
if we clearly understand what is being asked of us, our chances of
success are much greater? So it is with the boundaries you set for
your team of people who will just listen!

As my journey of grief continued for months after the death
of my wife, I became more acquainted with being at home alone,
although I never genuinely liked it. As I continued sharing my
emotions with the inner circle of "listeners," I realized being at
home alone held the potential for self-isolation—which was the
opposite of my personality—and my grief was taking me down
that path. I knew isolation could lead to depression, so to combat
this, I intentionally sought out conversation and connection. I
found a healthy balance, but it took time and caring people to
walk with me. I believe if you are intentional in developing a team

of people who will just listen—*the ministry of presence*—new friendships develop, and at a depth that will only be appreciated in retrospect.

The Blessing of Delegation

I (Rick) found in my early stages of grief that motivation was a foreign concept for me and many others who take this journey. The first week after Susie died, returning to simple tasks like mowing the lawn was beyond my scope of ability. After the first pass of the mower with a perfectly cut line, I was done! The following day I came out, the mower was in the same location where I'd left it, and I mowed another strip. Once again, I was done for the day! It wasn't until the third day that I finished my small lawn.

Mowing my lawn was not the only chore I struggled with, so a group of friends from church started showing up to do yardwork on a weekly basis. My group of friends also managed the needs of my sister-in-law, who had a physical disability due to her post-polio and lived alone at the time. They took care of all her outside chores, such as gardening, taking out the trash, minor repairs, and so on for weeks until I regained the motivation to assume my responsibilities at her house and mine. This was an incredible expression of love by my friends.

You may have friends who voluntarily show up to help, and you may have friends who say, "What can I do to help?" For both groups, think of simple tasks you lack the motivation to accomplish and delegate these. Seldom do people offer without the intent to help, so with clear direction, honor them by letting them express their love in acts of service. In fact, if you ask one person to take the lead, then you can communicate to that person, who can then delegate to others. Keep it simple! Whether you are pre-need or at-need with end-of-life, developing a team of trusted people to help in some areas of life could be one of the wisest decisions you make.

Jeff's Story

In chapter five—Struggling with Sudden Death—I (Rick) introduced Jeff's story of losing his son, Kris, to suicide. I became part of Jeff's team of supporters, as did many others. Jeff quickly adapted to this and benefited.

> *I (Jeff) surrounded myself with people I trusted and would help me. My church loved me with open arms, which included funding for extended grief counseling that was desperately needed. My church family gave us money to help with the burial cost. Friends helped with funeral arrangements, such as the video and pictures for the service. This collection of help from loving individuals was a significant part of my recovery—but I didn't fully appreciate or understand this until months and years later.*

As Jeff and I talked, I asked him to share how he walks out his ongoing recovery. "It's a daily and weekly step. I still feel the pain when there are family gatherings. When asked if I have kids, I say, 'Yes, I have a son who has passed by taking his own life.' This is how I emotionally deal with it: truth. I've learned to accept it." When asked what advice he can share with others, Jeff was clear in his response: "Take the time you need to grieve, rather than just moving on. Seek counseling. Don't think you are alone in the struggle because there are support groups and many others that have a shared experience."

There are stages to recovery, and understanding each stage is important. Jeff found journaling to be helpful. Journaling can provide an outlet for releasing your guilt, pain, anger, and sadness, which will be intense at first. It will allow you to process those feelings and say what you feel while eliminating judgment from anyone. This can help you move through those feelings.

> *(Jeff) In the beginning it was difficult, but it truly helped with reaching the depths of my emotions*

and releasing them to a place that was private and intimate and relieving somehow. I also learned the value of participating in support groups because you can become stuck at times, and although you feel stuck, you can get through this. I found tremendous support through a national group that deals with survivors of suicide. Most importantly, I learned how important it is to support your spouse and family. Take this journey together.

Resources

Where do you go for help? The list below covers a broad range of grief support groups and organizations that focus on grief. Some organizations have a defined focus, while others cover the subject of grief on a much broader scale. If you are looking for help, consider one or more of the groups listed in addition to professional help through a therapist, chaplain, priest, pastor, minister, rabbi, or another trained person.

- ACCESS (Air-Craft Casualty Emotional Support Services) Air disaster bereavement support network
  http://www.accesshelp.org
- Alive Alone
  www.alivealone.org
- American Foundation for Suicide Prevention
  https://afsp.org/
- Bereaved Parents of the USA
  www.bereavedparentsusa.org
- Center for Loss and Renewal
  www.lossandrenewal.com
- CLIMB (Center for Loss in Multiple Birth, Inc.)
  www.climb-support.org
- Compassionate Friends
  (Support for families who have lost a child)
  www.compassionatefriends.org
- First Candle
  (SIDS information and coping with the death of a baby)

www.firstcandle.org
- Grief Haven
  www.griefhaven.org
- Griefnet.org
  www.griefnet.org
- Parents of Murdered Children
  www.pomc.com
- SIDS
  www.mayoclinic.com/health/sudden-infant-death-syndrome/DS00145/DSECTION=coping-and-support
- Survivors of Suicide
  www.survivorsofsuicide.com
- The National Center for Grieving Children and Families
  www.dougy.org
- Tragedy Assistance Program for Survivors
  www.taps.org
- Twinless Twins
  www.twinlesstwins.org

(Kathryn) Always remember that no matter how bad you feel, you will survive. Basically, you have two choices: You can run from the feeling of grief, or you can face your loss, feel your feelings, and move through your grief to a new normal. You can carry your wound through life, or you can engage in ways to heal. It truly is a choice, and the choices we make today determine the choices we can make tomorrow. Remember, your grief journey will take as long as it takes. Your healing is unique and as individual as you are. Discouragement is normal. You will have days where you feel like you cannot take another sad, serious, teary, and confused day. You may even feel that your grieving journey will never end. These are normal feelings. Your job is to take care of yourself and love yourself while on your journey to recovery.

Action Steps

- Begin making a list of tasks you would like to delegate and ask someone for help.
- Develop a list of people to be on your team of "listeners." Reach out to one or two of them this week.
- Schedule a check-up with your doctor to discuss both your emotional and physical health.
- Review the websites listed in this chapter and research a local counselor.

Now It's Time!

W riting this book has caused me to reflect on the last twenty-eight years, which have included a myriad of events: my wife's cancer diagnosis; going back to school at age forty-four; transitioning from owning my own business to full-time vocational ministry; my wife's cancer treatment for the second and third time; the eventual end-of-life for my brother, wife, mom, and dad; grieving; and finding love again. What have I learned through all these events? Have a plan! As I say in chapter two, "Plan your dive and dive your plan" became one of my biggest allies. Why?

> Because with a systematic approach in preparing for end-of-life, your survivors will inherit your plan instead of your problems, allowing them to grieve in a healthy way as your wishes are carried out.

In the following appendices, I've put together some valuable resources to assist you in taking the next steps on your journey. One of them is a "Survivor Checklist©." I'd like to share an email I received from my friend and contributor Timothea "TJ" after I asked for her opinion about the checklist.

> *Hi Rick,*
> *I've never cried over a checklist before . . . until now. My husband, Ed, has been asking me lately, "Where's the life insurance? Where's the will/trust?*

*How would I ever put everything together and know
how to survive? You do it all! The finances, that is."
So, we set a date for each Saturday. Just an hour,
so he can get used to my system of doing things,
find the important papers, and know where all those
important passwords are hiding. He does the grunt
work . . . cars, yards, the heavy lifting sort of stuff.
So, he agreed to show me the ropes little by little—
like how to trip the breaker when the power shuts
down! All the stuff we longtime married couples
(thirty-four years this Saturday!) just don't pay real
attention to because we've done this dance for so
long. We're a team. I was thinking if he passed, or
I did before him, my team would be broken. Cut
in two. We work like a well-oiled machine. And I
started to cry just thinking that this wonderful man-
uscript is going to help so many people.*

Perhaps TJ's story sounds a lot like yours, except you have yet
to start working with your significant other to learn more about the
"rhythm" around your house. If so, what and when are you going
to change? Change is hard but not impossible! It takes adjustments
to not only accommodate change but also excel with it. What small
adjustment can you start with?

My encouragement to you is this: If you have the time and
ability to plan pre-need, start by having a conversation with your
family, using this book as your guide. If possible, have them also
read the book so that everyone can understand the same information, talk the same language, and have the same goal—to meet
your desires for end-of-life.

I leave you with this final thought. At the beginning of the
book, I shared the words of a person who called me immediately
after the death of her spouse, saying, "What do I do now? We were
supposed to be together forever! We didn't plan on one of us dying
and leaving the other." Hopefully, the information in this book
has equipped you to know what to do now. Take control, invest
the time, and complete your plan. You can do this. Now it's time!

APPENDIX A

Survivor Checklist©

One week after my wife, Susie, passed away, I sat at my kitchen table with my attorney, tax preparer, and financial advisor. "If I paid you $10,000 to manage all of this, would you do it?" I asked. It was a rhetorical question since I didn't have an extra $10,000 to spend. But I was so overwhelmed by what needed to be done that had they taken me up on the offer, I gladly would have paid! As wonderful as it would be to pay someone to manage your affairs so you could grieve and spend more time with your family, most of us don't have the extra funds for this luxury. So, now I use a Survivor Checklist©, which is a tool I developed after managing the affairs of my loved ones for guiding friends, parishioners, and families I meet with preparing to officiate their loved one's funeral or memorial. It is difficult to think clearly and pragmatically after the death of a loved one, so having a step-by-step approach will help you to prioritize and stay organized. The primary aim is to help you gather and document all the pertinent information that will be needed at the time of a loved one's end-of-life.

Whether you are planning for end-of-life or handling affairs at-need after a death has just occurred, this checklist is your starting point. In either case, the information required is the same. The only difference is the *immediacy* of the process. If you are operating in an at-need situation, remember the importance of building your team. The help of your family members, trusted friends, and professionals will be invaluable during this time. Also, keep in mind that you can relieve any team member of their "duties" at any time.

BUILD YOUR TEAM

Below is the Survivor Checklist©. You can download the Survivor Checklist© and a copy of the diagram above at www.WhenItsTime.org. Keep in mind that these are merely suggestions. Please consult with an attorney or financial advisor before taking any action.

To Do Immediately following Death:

Personal

- ❑ Notify immediate family members and close friends.
- ❑ Notify your employer and the deceased's employer and arrange for bereavement time off.
- ❑ If you or an immediate family member is a student, contact the school, teacher, or professor and inform them of

the death. This will allow for arrangements to be made for homework or tests to be taken later.

To Do Two to Three Days following Death:

Funeral/Memorial

- ❏ Contact funeral homes for interviews, then make arrangements for burial/cremation and request certified copies of the death certificate.
- ❏ Enlist the help of others to begin planning a funeral or memorial service.
- ❏ Ask a friend or family member to create a list of hotels and restaurants in the immediate area for out-of-town guests.
- ❏ Notify out-of-town relatives and friends as soon as possible so they can make plans for travel and time off work for the funeral or memorial.

Legal

- ❏ Locate any will or trust documents of the deceased.
- ❏ Contact the attorney who prepared the above documents.

Financial

- ❏ Contact the bank or financial institution where the deceased held individual or joint accounts. Locate recent bank statements on all individual and joint accounts that show account balances on the day or month of death.
- ❏ Notify credit card companies of the death if accounts are held in the deceased's name. If the credit card is held jointly, find out what documentation is required to change cards into the survivor's name. Note: Some credit card accounts may include a life insurance policy.

Insurance

- ❑ Locate all life insurance policies and review to see if they include death benefits that may help pay for related expenses.
- ❑ Contact all life insurance companies where the deceased had policies. Request a claim form or ask for help from the local agent. Decide whether to receive the benefit in a lump sum or have the money paid out over a designated time frame. There could be tax implications in either case, so consult with your insurance agent, financial advisor, or attorney to find out which method would be most beneficial for you.
- ❑ Contact the deceased's employer and inquire about any life insurance policies the employer provides. It is common for an employer to offer the employee a life insurance policy to cover all or part of the funeral costs.
- ❑ Contact the deceased's health insurance companies (medical, dental, vision) to notify them of the death.

Benefits

- ❑ File for Social Security benefits by contacting the Social Security Administration at 1-800-772-1213. Benefits may include a one-time benefit of $255 to the surviving spouse or dependent children. Check with your funeral director to determine what claims may have already been filed for you.
- ❑ If the deceased is a veteran, contact the Department of Veterans Affairs (VA) and inquire about burial costs covered by the VA and the process involved in submitting a claim. Claim forms can be completed online or at a veterans hospital, the funeral home, or the cemetery. Contact your funeral director or local Veteran Services Officer to determine if benefits may have already been filed for you. For Burial Benefits, call 1-800-827-1000. For Burial Headstone and Markers, call 1-800-697-6947.

Property

❑ If the deceased was living alone, contact the post office to have mail forwarded. This will prevent mail from accumulating and attracting attention. It can also inform you about creditors, subscriptions, and other accounts that need to be canceled.

To Do Two to Three Weeks following Death:

Property

❑ Change all utilities from the deceased's name. This could include gas, electric, water, garbage, phone, cable, internet, and so on.

Financial

❑ Contact the bank or financial institution where the deceased had a loan and inform them of the death. This could include a mortgage, student loan, car loan, and so on. They will be able to inform you if the loan was covered by credit life insurance and what needs to be done to file the appropriate claim (a death certificate is often required). Credit life insurance is designed to pay off a specific debt of the insured in the event of death. (This type of insurance also covers specific debt in the case of unemployment, disability, or illness.)

❑ Contact all sources of income that the deceased was receiving (investments, retirement accounts, Social Security) and apply for any funds/dividends that are due to you. You may need a certified copy of the death certificate for this. When contacting Social Security, have a conversation about retiring the deceased's Social Security number to prevent identity theft.

❑ Contact the major credit bureaus (Equifax, Experian, and TransUnion) to assist you in transferring your loved one's credit into your name after you seek counsel from your tax preparer or attorney. They may also be able to assist you in determining any outstanding obligations of the deceased.

❑ Contact your tax preparer. A tax return will need to be filed for the deceased and a return for his or her estate if applicable.

Insurance

❑ File life insurance claim form(s) with a certified copy of the death certificate. If you need any help, your funeral director or attorney can assist you. When filling out the claim form, you should have the following information available:
  ❑ The policy number(s) and face amounts
  ❑ The full name and address of the deceased
  ❑ Documentation of the deceased's date and place of birth
  ❑ Date, place, and cause of death
  ❑ Deceased's occupation and last date worked
  ❑ Claimant's name, age at death, and Social Security number

Property

❑ Contact the Department of Motor Vehicles (DMV) to retire the deceased's driver's license and change the titles and registrations of his or her vehicle(s).
❑ Cancel email, social media, and other online accounts to avoid fraud or identity theft. The procedures for each website will vary.

Personal

- ☐ Create a list of jobs to delegate to trusted friends and neighbors who ask, "What can I do to help?" Here are a few suggestions:
  - ☐ Yardwork
  - ☐ Drive kids to/from school
  - ☐ Prepare meals for you and your family
  - ☐ Run simple errands

To Do as Time Permits:

Financial

- ☐ Change joint accounts into the survivor's name *only once all checks for the deceased have been received and deposited.* Closing a financial account where the deceased is named too early could prevent final checks from being deposited. Survivors are typically advised to wait six months to a year before removing the decedent's name from bank accounts.

Insurance

- ☐ Review your own insurance needs, as these will often change after the death of a family member.

Property

- ☐ Consider removing the deceased's name from the deed on your property. This is done at the county seat where the property is located. You will need a certified copy of the death certificate for this.

Personal

- ☐ Reach out for counseling or grief support.

❑ Inform your physician about the recent loss of your loved one and schedule a check-up if needed. It's common to neglect your own health or fall behind on treating personal conditions during the season following a loss.

At-A-Glance

People to Notify of Death:
Employer or school (for deceased & survivors)
Attorney
Accountant
Financial Advisor
Physician (for deceased & survivors)
Life Insurance Company
Health Insurance Companies (medical/dental/vision)
Credit Card Companies
DMV

Documentation to Collect:
Death Certificate
Will and Trust Documents
Life Insurance Policies
Investment Fund Accounts
Health Insurance Policies
Birth Certificate
Driver's License
Passport
Military Discharge Papers DD214 Form (if veteran)

APPENDIX B

Order of Service Templates

Having officiated numerous funerals, memorials, graveside services, and burials at sea, I have found the order of service, which is the chronological flow of events, can vary depending upon the surviving family's personal convictions, cultural norms, and desires. To list all potential orders of services is not possible due to the potential variations, but I can offer two sample templates that can be altered to meet your need. If you are designing a service without the assistance of a funeral director, leader from your house of worship, or experienced family member or friend, then I encourage you to examine and explore the main service components: prayer, photographs/video, music, officiant's message, guest speakers, open microphone time, and conclusion. Use these service components as a general guideline—but they can change to meet your needs. This will assist you in a "flow" that ties the service together. Think of flow as a good rhythm that will help keep the attendees' interest and participation.

Sample Order of Service—Memorial or Funeral
(With Optional Graveside Service)

Name of deceased:	
Name of funeral director:	
Funeral venue:	
Funeral address:	
Date & time of funeral service:	
Name of officiant:	

If applicable:

Graveside venue:	
Graveside address:	
Date & time of graveside service:	

Service start time: 11:00 a.m. (example)
Total run time: 45–60 min.

Duration	Component
30 min.	Pre-service music & photo slideshow
1–2 min.	Officiant welcomes family and attendees
10–15 min.	Officiant offers first part of message
3–5 min.	Guest speaker #1
3–5 min.	Guest speaker #2
3–5 min.	Guest speaker #3
10–15 min.	Open mic (keep to 1–3 min per person)

8–10 min.	Officiant completes message
5–10 min.	Funeral director closes casket (if opened during service), and pallbearers move casket to waiting vehicle (for graveside service, if applicable).

Sample Order of Service—Graveside

Name of deceased:	
Name of funeral director:	
Graveside venue:	
Graveside address:	
Date & time of service:	
Name of officiant:	

Service start time: 12:30 p.m. (example)
Total run time: 30–35 min.

Duration	Component
7–10 min.	Hearse arrives from funeral home. Pallbearers are given instructions on how to remove the casket from the hearse and place it above the grave on a pre-arranged stand. Pallbearers then remove their gloves and place them on top of the casket. (If military or law enforcement, this may vary slightly)
1–2 min.	Officiant welcomes family and attendees
5–7 min.	Officiant offers first part of message. If there are no guest speakers, officiant may increase this time to 12–15 minutes.
3–5 min.	Guest speaker #1 (optional)

3–5 min.	Guest speaker #2 (optional)
3–5 min.	Guest speaker #3 (optional)
3–5 min.	Officiant completes message

Contributors

Barrie Sandy has served families in the financial services industry for twenty years. He is a licensed agent in California and the owner of Sandy Insurance Agency in Vallejo, consulting with customers on home, auto, and life insurance needs. Barrie also specializes in business insurance, providing coverage solutions for his clientele. He graduated from Pacific Christian College and lives in Napa, California.

Kent Kuhlmann has been a financial advisor/wealth manager for thirty years. Kent's company is a premier wealth management practice. He excels in financial and life insurance planning for clients throughout the country. Kent is an active board member of local firms advising and supporting the community of Napa. Kent lives in Napa, California, with his wife, Jennifer, and their son, Bodhi.

Rena Robinson has been a registered nurse for over twenty-five years. Rena's clinical experience includes geriatric care, skilled nursing facilities, assisted living facilities, higher education, clinical staff training, palliative care, and hospice care. She received her nursing degree from Eastern Kentucky University and also attended the University of Kentucky for nursing, clinical leadership and management, and higher education. Rena resides in Beaufort, South Carolina.

Phil Handley's life journey of helping others started in the US Coast Guard and then progressed into a career in the fire service, where he retired as a captain. He volunteered as a community chaplain with the Law Enforcement and Fire Chaplaincy of Napa County, responding to trauma, assisting with death notifications, and comforting families, witnesses, and first responders. Phil still lives in the community he served, Napa, California.

Steven Paris has been in law enforcement for over twenty-one years. He has served in correction, patrol, investigations, court services, and has been assigned as a coroner's investigator for over four years. His death-investigation training ranges from basic death investigation to the recovery of buried skeletal remains and forensic fire death investigation. Steven lives in California.

John T. Armstrong Jr, MD, MS, has a master's degree in cell biology and is a licensed obstetrician/gynecologist, practicing in Napa, California, for forty-one years. He completed his internship and residency at the UCSF Valley Medical Center. He is a member of the American Association of Physicians and Surgeons and an active staff member at Queen of the Valley Hospital. He lives in Napa, California.

Ken Graham has over sixteen years in the funeral industry as a funeral director and has served over 2,000 families. Ken is often told it is his compassion and patience with families that allow him to excel at his job. Ken attended Colorado University and is an Air Force veteran. He and his wife, Gilda, live in Suisun City, California.

Timothea "TJ" Galoner is an independent insurance agent who has specialized in the health and life insurance industries for over a decade. She carries multiple credentials based in Medicare, individual family health, and life insurance. TJ is a graduate of The Way Leadership University with high honors. TJ lives in San Bernardino, California, with her husband, Ed, and son, Nathaniel.

Kathryn Denham is a licensed clinical social worker who has been working as a Christian counselor in private practice for the past thirty years, specializing in grief, couples, families, addiction, teens, and children therapy. She grew up in Missouri and received her bachelor's degree at Harding Christian College in Arkansas and her master's degree at Kansas University. Kathryn lives in Vacaville, California.

Acknowledgments

A book spanning numerous topics under one theme, end-of-life, can only find its culmination from collaborative work. I am blessed to call so many people friends, and this collection of lifelong friends have given you and me a gift. Their shared experience will help you to enhance your legacy pertaining to end-of-life.

My Wife

Lauren Craig, you have been my prayer partner and encourager. It was the Lord who prompted me to write a book. You embraced that calling with support then, and it has not stopped. I wish everyone could feel as loved and supported as I do. Thank you, and I love you.

Contributors

I thank each one of you for helping me make this vision a reality. As each of you gave of your time and knowledge, you were being used by our Creator, who set me on this path. I am forever grateful!

Barrie Sandy, thank you for sharing your industry knowledge and passion to help people. You are a gifted communicator. I am grateful for your friendship over the last seventeen years, which includes praying for one another, and now collaboration on this book!

Kent Kuhlmann, you have been a financial planner and friend to me. I appreciate you sharing your expertise on estate planning and making yourself available anytime I wanted to talk.

Rena Robinson, your caring nature and loving spirit are qualities I love about you. Both of those qualities came out in your writing. You are treasured and appreciated.

Dr. John Armstrong, for well over twenty years, we have laughed, prayed, and supported one another. I am grateful for your friendship and contribution to my book. Let's keep playing pranks on one another!

Phil Handley, you are an incredible friend! If friendship was measured by the way a person supports someone else, then you are the definition of it. Thank you for the years of support. I love your family and look forward to many more years of friendship.

Steven Paris, I recognized the compassion you have for people as soon as we met. Your choice of words, body language when talking about helping people, and faith and commitment to your profession are exceptional. I am proud to know you, and I am grateful for your contribution to this book. Thank you, my friend.

Ken Graham, your story about why you became a funeral director is worthy of being a book. Your passion for your profession—serving others in their time of need—is what I respect most about you. Thank you for always answering my questions, contributing as an author, and being a friend. You are a gift!

Kathryn Denham, I love your sweet spirit. You make me and everyone around you feel calm and content. Thank you for your insight into the grief journey and your authorship in this book. I am blessed to know you.

Lon Dreyer, I always enjoy my time with you. I am grateful for who you are and the care you show families we work with. Your availability to answer questions I have and in-depth knowledge of the funeral industry has proven invaluable. Our friendship is special to me. Thank you.

Timothea "TJ" Galoner, your prayers, insight, and knowledge of your industry have been a constant encouragement to me. Your willingness to tell me "like it is" has been a fresh reminder that people care about this book and me enough to share truth. Thank you, my friend!

Interviews

Cassie McKee, asking you to relive one of the hardest parts of your life was difficult, but you answered the calling and shared your experience for the readers of this book. I am forever grateful and treasure our friendship then and today. Thank you.

Carolyn Skinner, thank you for sharing your life experience with such honesty and boldness, draped in humility and faith in our Lord. Your faith has helped me increase my faith. Thank you for sharing your story.

Jeff Roberts, you have played so many important roles in my life: prayer partner, mentor, church leader, and lifelong friend. Having you share your story in this book proves to me that you want to help others, and your courage to do so is proof of that. Grace and peace to you, my friend.

Editing and Guidance

Sarah Barnum, of TrailBlaze Writing & Editing, the only thing I would change about us working together is—it should have happened one year earlier. Your expertise and personality made me look forward to every one of your emails and suggestions. Thank you is not enough. Grateful is how I feel about you. Thank you.

Vicki Voitier, I am blessed to have a mother-in-law who is so fun to be around. You have been such a contributor to this book with editing and suggestions. I have loved our time together sharing opinions, debating over the details, and now, succeeding together. Thank you for your countless hours, love, and support.

Dr. Bill Mathis, as a licensed psychologist with professional experiences ranging from clinical psychology and private practice therapy to working for local and state government officials as well as the CIA and FBI, your expertise and experience amaze me. Most importantly for me, though, is that you have been a confidant, friend, and mentor personally and for this book. Thank you, Dr. Bill!

Administrative

Rob Voitier, without your efforts in gaining written permission to use others' literary work, there would be a void in this book. I am grateful for your contribution to this book and my life as a father-in-law.

Creative: Website and Book Design

Erik Bjarnason, you are a creative, intelligent, caring person who has a gift for articulating your thoughts. I am so thankful for your upbeat personality, insight into life, and willingness to work together on this project to develop my website and graphics. I am grateful for having you in my life.

Thank you, *Shawn Montoya*, for being part of this book in a very artistic way. I look forward to using more of your artwork with my next book. You are an incredible photographer, as people can see with the front cover.

Endnotes

Chapter 3—Giving the Gift of Organ Donation

1. "Organ Procurement Organizations (OPOs)," HRSA, last reviewed April 2021, https://www.organdonor.gov/get-involved/volunteer.
2. "National Donate Life Registry," Donate Life, accessed October 10, 2019, https://registerme.org/.
3. "The American Association of Tissue Banks," accessed October 10, 2019, https://www.aatb.org/.
4. "The Basic Path of Donation," Organ Procurement and Transplantation Network, U.S. Department of Health and Human Services, accessed October 10, 2019, https://optn.transplant.hrsa.gov/learn/about-donation/the-basic-path-of-donation/.
5. "How Organ Allocation Works," Organ Procurement and Transplantation Network, U.S. Department of Health and Human Services, accessed October 10, 2019, https://optn.transplant.hrsa.gov/learn/about-transplantation/how-organ-allocation-works/.
6. "Donor Matching System," Organ Procurement and Transplantation Network, U.S. Department of Health and Human Services, accessed October 10, 2019, https://optn.transplant.hrsa.gov/learn/about-transplantation/donor-matching-system/.
7. "Member Directory," Organ Procurement and Transplantation Network, U.S. Department of Health and Human Services, accessed October 10, 2019, https://optn.transplant.hrsa.gov/members/member-directory/.
8. "Organ Donation FAQ," Organ Procurement and Transplantation Network, U.S. Department of Health and Human Services, accessed October 10, 2019, https://www.organdonor.gov/learn/faq.
9. "Organ Donation and Religion," Donate Life America, accessed September 15, 2021, https://www.donatelife.net/organ-donation-and-religion/.
10. "Amish," Donate Life America, accessed September 15, 2021, https://www.donatelife.net/organ-donation-and-religion/#amish.

11. "Assembly of God," Donate Life America, accessed September 15, 2021, https://www.donatelife.net/organ-donation-and-religion/#assembly-of-god.
12. "Baptist," Donate Life America, accessed September 15, 2021, https://www.donatelife.net/organ-donation-and-religion/#baptist.
13. "Buddhism," Donate Life America, accessed September 15, 2021, https://www.donatelife.net/organ-donation-and-religion/#buddhism.
14. "Catholicism," Donate Life America, accessed September 15, 2021, https://www.donatelife.net/organ-donation-and-religion/#catholicism.
15. "Christian Science," Donate Life America, accessed September 15, 2021, https://www.donatelife.net/organ-donation-and-religion/#christian-science.
16. "Disciples of Christ," Donate Life America, accessed September 15, 2021, https://www.donatelife.net/organ-donation-and-religion/#disciples-of-christ.
17. "Episcopal," Donate Life America, accessed September 15, 2021, https://www.donatelife.net/organ-donation-and-religion/#episcopal.
18. "Evangelical Covenant Church," Donate Life America, accessed September 15, 2021, https://www.donatelife.net/organ-donation-and-religion/#evangelical.
19. "Greek Orthodox," Donate Life America, accessed September 15, 2021, https://www.donatelife.net/organ-donation-and-religion/#greek-orthodox.
20. "Hinduism," Donate Life America, accessed September 15, 2021, https://www.donatelife.net/organ-donation-and-religion/#hinduism.
21. "Islam," Donate Life America, accessed September 15, 2021, https://www.donatelife.net/organ-donation-and-religion/#islam.
22. "Judaism," Donate Life America, accessed September 15, 2021, https://www.donatelife.net/organ-donation-and-religion/#judaism.
23. "Lutheran Church," Donate Life America, accessed September 15, 2021, https://www.donatelife.net/organ-donation-and-religion/#lutheran.
24. "Mennonite," Donate Life America, accessed September 15, 2021, https://www.donatelife.net/organ-donation-and-religion/#mennonite.
25. "(Mormon) Church of Jesus Christ of Latter-day Saints," Donate Life America, accessed September 15, 2021, https://www.donatelife.net/organ-donation-and-religion/#mormon.
26. "Presbyterian," Donate Life America, accessed September 15, 2021, https://www.donatelife.net/organ-donation-and-religion/#presbyterian.
27. "Sikh," Donate Life America, accessed September 15, 2021, https://www.donatelife.net/organ-donation-and-religion/#sikh.
28. "Southern Baptist Convention," Donate Life America, accessed September 15, 2021, https://www.donatelife.net/organ-donation-and-religion/#southern-baptist-convention.
29. "United Methodist," Donate Life America, accessed September 15, 2021, https://www.donatelife.net/organ-donation-and-religion/#methodist.

Chapter 4—Receiving Hospice Care

1. "The History of Hospice Care and Palliative Care," Family Comfort Hospice and Palliative Care, accessed September 15, 2021, https://familycomforthospice.org/the-history-of-hospice-care-and-palliative-care/.
2. "Choosing and Finding the Right Hospice Care for You," CaringInfo, National Hospice and Palliative Care Organization, accessed September 15, 2021, https://www.caringinfo.org/types-of-care/hospice-care/choosing-and-finding-hospice-care/.
3. "Hospice Care," CaringInfo, National Hospice and Palliative Care Organization, accessed September 15, 2021, https://www.caringinfo.org/types-of-care/hospice-care/.
4. "Choosing and Finding the Right Hospice Care for You," CaringInfo, National Hospice and Palliative Care Organization, accessed September 15, 2021, https://www.caringinfo.org/types-of-care/hospice-care/choosing-and-finding-hospice-care/.
5. "The 4 Common Myths About Hospice Care," VeryWell Health, updated October 10, 2020, https://www.verywellhealth.com/hospice-care-4014065.

Chapter 6—Coping with Miscarriage, Stillbirth, and Infant Loss

1. "Miscarriage Burial Laws," Office of Legislative Research, written January 11, 2018, www.cga.ct.gov/2018/rpt/pdf/2018-R-0032.pdf.
2. "Disposition of Fetal Remains," The General Assembly of Pennsylvania House Bill No. 1890, referred to committee on health September 26, 2019, https://www.legis.state.pa.us/CFDOCS/Legis/PN/Public/btCheck.cfm?txtType=PDF&sessYr=2019&sessInd=0&billBody=H&billTyp=B&billNbr=1890&pn=2623.

Chapter 7—Clarifying Bereavement Leave

1. "A Guide to Bereavement Leave," Employment Law Handbook, accessed September 14, 2020, https://www.employmentlawhandbook.com/resources/a-guide-to-bereavement-leave/.

Chapter 11—Applying for Veterans Benefits

1. "Eligibility for Burial in a VA National Cemetery," U.S. Department of Veterans Affairs, last updated March 18, 2021, https://www.va.gov/burials-memorials/eligibility/.
2. "Pre-need Eligibility for Burial in a VA Cemetery," U.S. Department of Veterans Affairs, last updated April 5, 2021, https://www.va.gov/burials-memorials/pre-need-eligibility/.
3. "About Funerals," Arlington National Cemetery, accessed September 14, 2019, https://www.arlingtoncemetery.mil/Funerals/About-Funerals.

4. "Burial at Sea," MyNavy HR, accessed September 14, 2019, https://www.mynavyhr.navy.mil/Support-Services/Casualty/Mortuary-Services/Burial-at-Sea/.
5. "Schedule a Burial for a Veteran or Family Member," U.S. Department of Veterans Affairs, last updated April 30, 2020, https://www.va.gov/burials-memorials/schedule-a-burial/.
6. "How to Apply for a Veterans Burial Allowance," U.S. Department of Veterans Affairs, last updated July 1, 2021, https://www.va.gov/burials-memorials/veterans-burial-allowance/.
7. "Burial Benefits," U.S. Department of Veterans Affairs, last updated May 28, 2021, https://www.cem.va.gov/burial_benefits/.
8. "How to Apply for a Veterans Burial Allowance," U.S. Department of Veterans Affairs, last updated July 1, 2021, https://www.va.gov/burials-memorials/veterans-burial-allowance/.
9. "Emblems of Belief," U.S. Department of Veterans Affairs, last updated August 18, 2021, https://www.cem.va.gov/cem/hmm/emblems.asp.
10. "Burial Flags to Honor Veterans and Reservists," U.S. Department of Veterans Affairs, last updated September 24, 2020, https://www.cem.va.gov/cem/burial_benefits/burial_flags.asp.

Chapter 12—Accessing Social Security Benefits

1. "Retirement Benefits," Social Security Administration, accessed September 14, 2019, https://www.ssa.gov/benefits/retirement/learn.html#h1.
2. "Social Security Credits," Social Security Administration, accessed September 14, 2019, https://www.ssa.gov/planners/credits.html.
3. "The Strangest Social Security Benefit You Can Get," The Motley Fool, created May 23, 2018, https://www.fool.com/retirement/2018/05/23/the-strangest-social-security-benefit-you-can-get.aspx.
4. "Overview of Our Disability Programs," Social Security Administration Red Book, accessed September 14, 2019, https://www.ssa.gov/redbook/eng/overview-disability.htm.

Chapter 13—Grieving Your Loss

1. GriefShare Ministry video seminar, episode 2, "Challenges of Grief," quote by Dr. Paul David Tripp at 30:48.
2. David Richo, *The 5 Things We Cannot Change* (Boulder: Shambhala, 2006), X1 and X11.
3. Billy Graham, *Death and the Life After* (Nashville: Thomas Nelson, 2011).

CPSIA information can be obtained
at www.ICGtesting.com
Printed in the USA
BVHW050202180323
660666BV00015B/545